NORBERT ELIAS

D0222918

Norbert Elias is one of the few twentieth-century sociologists recognized as ranking among the truly great and classical social thinkers. Between the 1930s, when he wrote what are now acclaimed as modern classics, *The Court Society* and *The Civilizing Process*, and the 1980s, he developed a unique approach to social theory known as figurational or process sociology. Since the translation of his work into English began to accelerate in the 1980s, a growing number of books and articles on topics including health, sexuality, gender, crime, national and ethnic identity and globalization, in a variety of disciplines, utilize Elias as an authority on the history of emotions, identity, the body, violence and state formation. Robert van Krieken's lucid book provides a concise, comprehensive critical guide which locates Elias's work clearly within both the historical development of sociology and contemporary debates, and identifies his contribution to the future directions of social theory and research.

Robert van Krieken is Senior Lecturer in Sociology at the University of Sydney.

KEY SOCIOLOGISTS

This series presents concise and readable texts covering the work, life and influence of many of the most important sociologists, and sociologically-relevant thinkers, from the birth of the discipline to the present day. Aimed primarily at the undergraduate, the books will also be useful to pre-university students and others who are interested in the main ideas of sociology's major thinkers.

Max Weber by Frank Parkin
Emile Durkheim by Kenneth Thompson
The Frankfurt School and its Critics by Tom Bottomore
Michel Foucault by Barry Smart
Erving Goffman by Tom Burns
Jürgen Habermas by Michael Pusey
Daniel Bell by Malcolm Waters

NORBERT ELIAS

Robert van Krieken

ROUTLEDGE

LONDON AND NEW YORK

First published 1998 by Routledge
11 New Fetter Lane, London EC4P 4EE

Simultaneously published in the USA and Canada
by Routledge
29 West 35th Street, New York, NY 10001

Typeset in Adobe Garamond and Scala Sans by Keystroke, Jacaranda
Lodge, Wolverhampton
Printed and bound in Great Britain by Clays Ltd, St Ives PLC

British Library Cataloguing in Publication Data
A catalogue record for this book is available from the British Library

Library of Congress Cataloguing in Publication Data
Van Krieken, Robert.
    Norbert Elias / Robert van Krieken.
      p.   cm.
    Includes bibliographical references and index.
    1. Elias, Norbert. 2. Sociologists—Germany—Biography.
  3. Sociology—Europe—Philosophy. I. Title.
  HM22.G8E559   1998
  301'.092—dc21   97–27714
                                                    CIP

ISBN 0–415–10415–7 (hbk)
ISBN 0–415–10416–5 (pbk)

Contents

ACKNOWLEDGEMENTS

I am indebted to Michael Pusey for encouraging me to get this project going in the first place, as well as Peter Hamilton and Chris Rojek for supporting it in its early stages. A number of people have painstakingly read and commented on all or part of the manuscript as it was being written: Eric Dunning, Johan Goudsblom, Stephen Mennell, Paul Nixon and Nico Wilterdink, and I am grateful for their encouragement and their assistance in helping me avoid some of the more glaring errors of fact and interpretation. Thanks, too, to Stefan Breuer, Bob Connell and George Ritzer for their supportive comments.

Others have corresponded or conversed with me in various ways during the writing of the book – responding to queries about his biography, providing me with relatively inaccessible pieces of Elias's work, and commenting on his relationship to other writers or schools of thought, and here I would like to thank Kenneth Anders, Jack Caldwell, Heike Hanna, Lisa Hill, Richard Kilminster, Nils Runeby, Pieter Spierenberg, Maggie Studholme and Saskia Visser. Hans-Peter Duerr has also been generous in passing on any material related to his critique of Elias, for which I am very grateful.

Alan Davis kindly provided detailed commentary on what life would have been like for Elias in pre-war Paris – 'Norby en Paris', as he affectionately put it. The book is the poorer for not having had the benefit of his critique of my stylistic clichés, not to mention his powerful general scepticism about any concept of 'evolutionary' social change.

The University of Sydney generously provided me with a period of leave in 1994 as part of its Special Studies Program, during which I undertook most of the research for the book and much of the writing.

Thanks to Alex for her support and encouragment.

I have used extensive quotations from one of Elias's books in particular, *The Civilizing Process*, and I am grateful to Basil Blackwell Ltd for generously giving me permission to do so.

ABBREVIATIONS

The following abbreviations are used in the references for Elias's major books.

CP *The Civilizing Process* (1994)
CS *The Court Society* (1983)
EO *The Established and the Outsiders* (1965)
ID *Involvement and Detachment* (1987)
RL *Reflections on a Life* (1994)
SI *The Society of Individuals* (1991)
TG *The Germans* (1996)
WiS *What is Sociology?* (1978)

1

INTRODUCTION

The kind of imagination best suited to life in the twenty-first century will be one which recognizes that we are also moving from one millennium to another. It will be enormously useful to draw on the work of thinkers whose perspectives are broader than a single decade or even a whole century, who ask questions emerging from a truly historical conception of social life. What does it actually mean to be a 'modern', 'civilized' person? How are we to understand the ways in which an understanding of our history can contribute to a more effective response to current human problems? Can we explain the contemporary world in terms of its genealogy, and where is it headed in the future? What is the significance of differing social configurations in producing particular kinds of human beings, who relate to each other, themselves and their social world in specific, often self-destructive ways? How is our concern with individual autonomy and independence related to the very real patterns of *interdependence* which characterize all human social life? These are the kinds of questions which Norbert Elias addressed for over half a century between the 1930s and the 1980s, developing a unique approach to sociology which is now beginning to take root in contemporary sociological research and theory.

Elias only began to be recognized as a major sociologist after the 1980s. He had an underground reputation in the 1950s among those of his English colleagues who could see the potential in his ideas, and a scattering of scholars in Europe who had managed to obtain a copy of his major work, *Über den Prozeß der Zivilisation*. In the 1960s, word gradually spread about the importance of his approach to sociology and history, primarily in the Netherlands and Germany, and then in France where his work began to be translated in the 1970s. In the United States, writers such as Erving Goffman and Reinhard Bendix referred to his work, but only in passing, for there was no English translation. For the same reason, English sociologists who had worked alongside him or been taught by him at the University of Leicester absorbed his ideas, but without identifying him as the source of crucial aspects of their sociological perspective. German students, in contrast, circulated photocopies of the expensive hardback edition of his book until it came out in paperback in 1976, and by 1993 Elias was the leading German publisher of Suhrkamp's bestseller.[1]

Since the translation of his work into English began to accelerate in the 1980s, a growing number of books and articles on topics including health, sexuality, crime, shame, national and ethnic identity, femininity and globalization, in a variety of disciplines, make positive reference to Elias as an authority on the history of emotions, identity, violence, the body and state formation. Lewis Coser referred to him as 'one of the most significant sociological thinkers of our day'[2] and Zygmunt Bauman described him as 'indeed a great sociologist'.[3] 'Long before American scholars had discovered the idea of historical sociology', wrote Christopher Lasch, 'Elias understood the possibilities of this new genre and worked them out with an imaginative boldness that still surpasses later studies in this vein.'[4] Anthony Giddens describes his work as 'an extraordinary achievement, anticipating issues which came to be generally explored in social theory only at a much later date'.[5] Elias's teaching, writing and ideas are gradually exercising an increasingly pervasive influence on an ever-widening circle of sociologists as well as a broader lay public, in an expanding number of countries and languages, and he is now starting to take his place in the sociology textbooks and dictionaries.[6]

His autonomy from the more fashionable trends in sociology contributed to his exclusion from sustained consideration as a sociological theorist, and it is both a source of appeal for those looking for something 'new' in sociology and a barrier to a balanced assessment of his ideas. Commentators tend to veer between two diametrically opposed poles, between uncritical acceptance or ungenerous rejection, so that debates on Elias's work frequently take on the character of theological disputes between supposedly admiring 'followers' and critics. However, to appreciate Elias most productively we need to steer a path between these two poles, towards a *critical* understanding of the contribution that his ideas can make to contemporary sociology. Elias offered a penetrating and novel analysis of the historical roots and development of modern society, forms of social interaction and social identity. It constituted a synthesis of the most advanced ideas in German, American, French and British social science up to the 1930s, integrating both different disciplinary perspectives and different national traditions. The result was a distinctive approach to sociology intended to *resolve* the major debates and disputes in social theory, rather than merely *rehearse* them, aimed at moving beyond disciplinary and national boundaries in social science rather than simply reproducing them. Whether or not we see Elias's work as constituting a transcendence of many of sociology's major conceptual and empirical obstacles, a robust engagement with the issues he raised can usefully inform the direction that sociological thought takes into the next millennium.

There are three interlinking principles guiding the discussion here which distinguish it from most treatments of Elias's work.

First, a critical approach will be taken to Elias's own assessments of his ideas. In other words, the possibility will be left open to use Elias to argue against Elias, subjecting his own work to the same kind of scrutiny he gave to that of others.

Second, I will not assume that his work formed a unified whole, and will look for possible contradictions, conflicts or tensions between different parts of his writings. Elias was disinclined ever to say he had changed his mind about anything. When a new idea or formulation emerged, he simply stopped using the earlier versions, with little explicit discussion of whether his line of thought had changed. Indeed, he had the irritating habit of presenting such developments in his thinking as mere 'clarifications' of 'misunderstandings' of his work, when he was actually referring to interpretations fairly faithful to his own formulations. A mistake made by both defenders and critics of Elias is to assume a simple unity to his work. In fact, it is frequently characterized by tensions and contradictions, and it is the working through of these tensions which makes his work interesting and important. The discussion of sociological theory is often characterized by fruitless debate arising from a refusal to acknowledge that a writer may have said different things at different times, with one commentator opposing the other with their version of the correct interpretation. This applies as much to Elias as it does to other major sociological thinkers.

Third, my initial premise in approaching both Elias's criticisms of others and critiques of Elias's work is that they are likely to have at least a kernel of truth, and that they rest on a *possible* interpretation of the ideas at issue. In other words, a 'principle of generosity' will apply, and my concern will be to identify how the interpretation was reached. This does not mean that I will refrain from arguing for alternative understandings to both Elias himself and his critics, but rather that I will be reluctant to suggest that either has got something entirely wrong.

I will outline both the *form* of sociological reasoning and enquiry that Elias argued for and continuously developed in his own research, and the *substantive* areas he explored – the historical development of what we experience as a particularly 'civilized' and self-disciplined identity and habitus, the part played by state formation in that development, the sociology of sport and leisure, social scientific knowledge, childhood and inter-generational relations, community formation and the dynamics of national identity-formation.

Elias offers a particular paradigm for sociological thought, one which opposes both the structural-functionalist and method-ological-individualist tendencies in sociology in a very different way from either the Marxist and neo-Marxist critics, or post-structuralist and postmodernist theorists. He developed a unique set of concepts for analysing social life which, he hoped, can cut through many of the central dilemmas in sociology, especially the apparent oppositions between action and structure, individual and society. Elias did not merely provide another solution to the problems of structure and agency and conflict versus consensus which have occupied the majority of sociologists for many decades. He argued for ways in which we might *dissolve* them as problems altogether, by avoiding the conceptual errors associated with the direction sociological thought took in being structured by Parsons' formulation of the so-called 'Hobbesian problem of order' (this will be examined in more detail in Chapter 3).

The substantive issues Elias dealt with – the history of emotions, attitudes towards the body, sexuality, socialization, and so on – anticipated later work such as that of Philippe Ariès, the French *Annales School* in history, Richard Sennett and Christopher Lasch, often providing a more systematic and effective approach to the same problems. His analysis of the historical development of emotions and psychological life is particularly important in relation to the connections he established with larger-scale processes such as state formation, urbanization and economic development.

There are at least five interconnected principles underlying Elias's approach to sociology. First, although societies are composed of human beings who engage in intentional action, the outcome of the combination of human actions is most often *unplanned* and *unintended*. The task for sociologists is, then, to analyse and explain the mechanics of this transformation of intentional human action into unintended patterns of social life, which necessarily takes place over longer or shorter periods of time.

A second, related, principle was that human individuals can only be understood in their *interdependencies* with each other, as part of networks of social relations, or what he often referred to as 'figurations'. Rather than seeing individuals as possessing an 'autonomous' identity with which they then interact with each other and relate to something we call a 'society', Elias argued that we are social to our very core, and only exist in and through our relations with others, developing a socially constructed 'habitus' or 'second nature'. An important subsidiary principle is that the study of processes of social development and transformation – what Elias called *sociogenesis* – is necessarily linked to the analysis of *psychogenesis* – processes of psychological development and transformation, the changes in personality structures or habitus which accompany and underlie social changes.

Third, human social life should be understood in terms of *relations* rather than *states*. For example, instead of power being a 'thing' which persons, groups or institutions possess to a greater or lesser degree, Elias argued we should think in terms of power relations, with ever-changing 'balances' or 'ratios' of power between individuals and social units.

Fourth, human societies can only be understood as consisting of long-term *processes* of development and change, rather than as timeless states or conditions. He spoke in this regard of the 'retreat of sociologists into the present'. Elias's sociology is above all a historical sociology, although he himself rejected the term, largely because he argued it should be assumed that sociology is undertaken historically, and such a term implies the possibility and legitimacy of a non-historical sociology. His point was more that sociologists cannot logically avoid concerning themselves with the diachrony of long-term social processes in order to understand current social relations and structures. Here he also anticipated the later development of historical sociology by writers such as Philip Abrams, Barrington Moore, Theda Skocpol and Charles Tilly.

Fifth, sociological thought moves constantly between a position of social and emotional *involvement* in the topics of study, and one of *detachment* from them. In contrast to natural science, the fact that sociologists study other interdependent human beings means that they are part of their object of scientific study, and thus cannot avoid a measure of involvement in their own research and theorizing. Social-scientific knowledge develops within the society it is part of, and not independently of it. At the same time, however, this involvement is often a barrier to an adequate understanding of social life, especially one which can resolve or transcend any of the persistent problems characterizing human beings' relationships with each other. The most obvious problem Elias was concerned with was violence. He felt it was important for social scientists to try to transcend the emotion-laden, everyday conceptualization of the human world and develop a 'way of seeing' that went beyond current ideologies and mythologies. Indeed, he often referred to sociologists as engaged in the 'destruction of myths'.

A number of other lines of argument flow from the application of these principles, such as the importance of state formation in analysing social development; a conception of science as a social institution; an emphasis on the relation between social change and psychological development, or as he called it, 'sociogenesis' and 'psychogenesis', often referred to as the relation between the micro and macro levels of sociological analysis; an interdisciplinary orientation to social science, interlinking above all sociology, psychology and history; an understanding of power relations as being frequently organized around the distinction between established and outsider groups. Taken together with the five underlying principles, these lines of argument form the basic framework of Elias's conception of sociological theory and research.

None of these concepts and points are entirely unique to Elias, and they can all be found in the work of other sociologists. However, what makes his approach so powerful is the combination or *synthesis* of what is currently spread across a variety of socio-logical perspectives – structuralism, symbolic interactionism, conflict theory, historical sociology, theories of the state and state formation. A number of commentators have spoken of the fragmentation of sociology as a discipline. What Elias offers is not a 'solution' to that problem, but a set of sensitizing concepts, an orientation to how one thinks about and practises sociology with the potential to draw many of the various threads of sociological thought together.

All of these principles and lines of argument in Elias's work interlink with each other, so that it is difficult to grasp adequately any single one or subset of them without attending to their inter-relationships with the others. In other words, in interpreting Elias's work it is important to refer to the relations between all the various strands, rather than taking any one of them in isolation. This does not mean that this book is a comprehensive survey of Elias's work. For that purpose it is, of course, far better to read Elias himself, or at least the lengthier treatment in Stephen Mennell's *Norbert Elias: An Introduction.*[7] Here the concern is more to provide a basic sketch of Elias's sociological perspective and his approach to sociological research, as well as to locate and position his ideas within broader sociological debates.

In an interview Norbert Elias once remarked on a comment that a reviewer, Zygmunt Bauman, had made on his work, that he was 'perhaps the last representative of classical sociology, someone striving after the great synthesis'. He said that this made him angry, because he 'would rather be the first one to open up a new path'.[8] This difference between Elias's self-understanding and the way many commentators have approached him captures an important feature of his work. Elias combines, on the one hand, a synthesis of the most powerful elements of late nineteenth- and early twentieth-century sociological thought with, on the other hand, a strongly independent and intellectually rigorous mobilization of that synthesis in relation to a wide range of empirical evidence.

Elias himself would not have used the term 'radical', but it may be the best way to describe his approach to sociology. At a time when most sociologists turned away from history and poured scorn on the dangers of evolutionism, he insisted on placing historical analysis and a concern with directional social development at the centre of sociological thought. He maintained a linkage between sociology and other human sciences such as psychology and history while the discipline became increasingly isolated and fragmented. He mounted a powerful argument against individualism, in favour of a self-discipline which resonates with the requirements of living as part of a group, throughout a period when concepts such as 'emancipation' and 'freedom' had worked their way to the heart of social science. He argued for the importance of transcending the boundaries of nation–states and thinking of terms of 'humanity as a whole' well before social scientists started using the term 'globalization'. His conceptualization of history in terms of long-term processes challenges, arguably more effectively than any of the existing critiques, the temporal divisions which plague social science, particularly that between 'tradition' and 'modernity', subjecting the self-assessment of 'modern' itself to critical analysis. This also means that he did not accept the notion that we have entered a 'postmodern' period; indeed, he preferred to describe us today as 'late barbarians'[9] living at the closing of the

Middle Ages. Like Bruno Latour,[10] Elias felt that 'we have never been modern', let alone become postmodern.

Right up to his death in 1990 at the age of 93, Elias thought about and practised sociology much as he lived his life, as an out-sider to the establishment. Although his ideas are increasingly becoming part of mainstream sociological thought, it seems likely that he would have continued to maintain a position of radical criticism of all those established orthodoxies he felt still stood in the way of a truly human society. This does not mean we should not be critical of many aspects of his work; we should, and I will discuss the main areas in which we can think about diverging from or developing Elias's positions. But whether we move with Elias, go 'beyond Elias' or identify alternative perspectives, engaging with his ideas usefully contributes to the development of more thoughtful and vigorous forms of sociological practice.

2

AN INTELLECTUAL SKETCH

Norbert Elias began his university studies in 1918, aged twenty-one, at the University of Breslau, which was then part of Germany. His major subjects were medicine and philosophy, with some of his philosophy semesters undertaken in Freiburg and Heidelberg, under Heinrich Rickert, Karl Jaspers and Edmund Husserl. It was in a seminar paper for the young Jaspers that he examined Thomas Mann's discussion of the relation between 'culture' and 'civilization', a theme he would return to later. In Breslau his philosophy teacher was the neo-Kantian Richard Hönigswald, who later became his doctoral supervisor. Like many ambitious university students, he found he 'could not ride two horses at once'[1] and dropped medicine – the preferred choice of his father, who wanted him to become a doctor – to concentrate on philosophy. However, later he recollected that his medical studies had a profound effect on both his approach to philosophy and his subsequent turn to sociology. It was the contrast between the philosophers' image of human beings as having an inner being of ideas and his medical experience of living tissue, brain structure and sense organs by which they constantly communicated with each other that led him to think of human beings as fundamentally interdependent. 'The discrepancy,' he wrote, 'between the philosophical, idealist image of man and the anatomical, physiological one unsettled me for many years'.[2]

This period of study began immediately after Elias's return from the war. He had entered military service in 1915, serving with a communications unit, at first in Poland and then on the Western front. Born on 22 June, 1897 in Breslau (now Wracłow in Poland), he was the only child of Hermann and Sophie Elias. His father was a textile manufacturer, and the family was relatively well-off, middle-class and Jewish. The young Norbert attended the humanist Johannes Gymnasium in Breslau between 1907 and 1914, where he first read the philosopher Immanuel Kant, as well as the classics of German literature, including Schiller, Goethe and Heine. At school he had developed both an ambition to become an academic, and an awareness that being Jewish meant it would not be an easy task. He later recalled having said in class when he was fifteen or sixteen that he wanted to become a university professor, and a classmate interrupting: '*That* career was cut off for you at birth'.[3]

Hönigswald was the second person – the first was his father – who Elias felt taught him how to think. Elias remembered him as authoritarian, intolerant of fools, passing fads and speculation, an implacable hard worker, who gave Elias 'the confidence that through reflection one may discover something new and something certain'.[4] There were four aspects of his writing of his DPhil dissertation – *Idee und Individuum: Eine Kritische Untersuchung zum Begriff der Geschichte*, completed in 1924 – which were crucial for his future sociological thought.

First, in the course of writing his thesis Elias, like many other scholars at the time and since, was influenced by Ernst Cassirer's[5] demonstration that scientists had moved from seeing the world in terms of *substances* to understanding it in terms of *relations*. Cassirer's philosophical understanding of relationism did not go far enough for Elias, because Cassirer still had an underdeveloped grasp of the *social* and *historical* contexts of the objects of scientific study. Cassirer, argued Elias later, continued to neglect precisely those concerns which define the field of sociology, 'dealing with real events, such as power struggles between human groups, such as cycles of violence . . . or with long-term social processes such as state formation processes, of knowledge growth, of urbanization, of population growth. . . '.[6] Nonetheless, it was through an encounter with the work of Cassirer that Elias developed the notion that:

> One must start by thinking about the structure of the whole in order to understand the form of the individual parts. These and many other phenomena have one thing in common, different as they may be in all other respects: *to understand them it is necessary to give up thinking in terms of single, isolated substances and to start thinking in terms of relationships and functions.*[7]

Reading Cassirer had a similar influence on a range of other thinkers, including Kurt Lewin, Edward Sapir, Claude Lévi-Strauss and, more recently, Pierre Bourdieu.

Second, in pursuing the implication of this point, Elias developed a profoundly critical attitude towards what he felt was *the* philosophical understanding of individual human beings, an understanding that, he argued, has continued to exert a powerful influence on sociological thought. In 1969 he wrote:

> The conception of the individual as *homo clausus*, a little world in himself who ultimately exists quite independently of the great world outside, determines the image of man in general. Every other human being is likewise seen as a *homo clausus*; his core, his being, his true self appears likewise as something divided within him by an invisible wall from everything outside, including every other human being.[8]

All his life Elias continued to argue against this conception of individuality and human identity, which he felt persisted in the structure of most sociological thought, despite the explicit acceptance of the apparently obvious argument that individual identity is socially constructed. We do not know if he read this passage in Marx, but Elias's position was essentially that of Marx's Sixth Thesis on Feuerbach: 'the human essence is no abstraction inherent in each single individual. In its reality it is the ensemble of the social relations'.[9]

Third, he developed an approach to ideas, thought and knowledge which he was later to apply both to personality structure and social life itself, namely that any given state of affairs can be understood as having arisen from an earlier stage, so that human thought can be seen *historically*, as consisting of stages, sequences or processes of development. As he wrote later, 'what I was dealing with in that form in 1922–24 was clearly – as it still is today – the peculiar order of long-term processes and their difference from the lawlike order of physical nature, as a kind of framework for human history'.[10]

Fourth, partly as a consequence of this line of thought, Elias had a serious falling-out with Hönigswald about aspects of his argument in the thesis, which resulted in Elias removing the offending passages so that Hönigswald would agree to allow the thesis to be submitted. The nature of the dispute is not entirely clear and the subject of intense debate.[11] Elias recalled that it concerned the Kantian notion of 'a priori truth' – categories of thought which are not simply derived from experience, but are necessary to apprehend experience. Elias felt that the neo-Kantians saw these core categories of thought as lying outside of society and history, as possessing an eternal validity of their own, and he stated that his criticisms of this conception was what Hönigswald objected to. 'I could no longer ignore the fact,' wrote Elias, 'that all that Kant regarded as timeless and as given prior to all experience, whether it be the idea of causal connections or of time or of natural and moral laws, together with the words that went with them, had to be learned from other people in order to be present in the consciousness of the individual human being'.[12]

However, Benjo Maso argues that this was a point which the neo-Kantians, including both Cassirer and Hönigswald, had themselves made, and suggests that it was impossible Hönigswald would have rejected the concept that categories of thought are learned. The problem may have been more complex, in that Elias wanted to go beyond saying that categories of thought were prior to experience, to analyse the social and historical formation of those categories. Maso's interpretation is that Hönigswald seems to have regarded that as an attack on the very notion of a prioris itself, which was such a central element of neo-Kantian philosophy that he could not accept Elias's position. It may also have been a case of mutual misunderstanding, in that Hönigswald simply wanted to maintain that the attempt to establish the validity of ideas *at all* was inherent in all human thought, so that although the *criteria* for establishing the validity of ideas were learned, the *principle* of validity (*Geltung*) was not, and he understood Elias to be arguing that it too was subject to historical variation.

In any event, the effect was that Elias had been cut off from any future career in philosophy, with no prospect of further support from Hönigswald as a supervisor of the German 'second doctorate', the *Habilitationsschrift*, required to obtain a permanent university post. On completing his dissertation at the age of twenty-six, his parents were in dire financial straits because of the effects of inflation on their savings, and he worked to support them for about two years in a metal goods factory, selling pipes. When the new Reichsmark helped bring inflation under control, his parents no longer required his help, and his thoughts returned to study. While Elias was in Heidelberg, Jaspers had spoken to him about Max Weber, and his experiences in the war and the factory had evoked a desire 'to get closer to a field of study connected to real life experience',[13] so a turn to sociology seemed the obvious step. He had sold some short stories to a newspaper, and anticipated he would be able to support himself as a journalist.

HEIDELBERG 1925–1929

In 1925, aged twenty-seven, he moved to Heidelberg, hoping that Max Weber's brother, Alfred Weber, would take him on for his *Habilitation*. It took him a while to formulate a topic, settling on the transition from prescientific to scientific thought, and travelled to Florence to examine documents on Galileo and the painters Masaccio and Uccello. Weber agreed in principle to supervise his thesis on the origins of the natural sciences in Florentine society, but Elias had to wait his turn, around four to five years. Nothing came of his journalistic ambitions, and he relied on his father's financial support. Another sociologist, the twenty-three-year-old Talcott Parsons, was also drawn to Heidelberg at the same time, starting his PhD on *The Concept of Capitalism in Recent German Literature*, although the two young men appear not to have met. Like many of their contemporaries, both understood that Heidelberg was close to being the very best place for a sociologist to work and study, attracting them with its powerful intellectual climate, based on a gathering of formidable intellects engaged in a lively and productive development of sociological thought.

He met and became friends with Karl Mannheim, who was four years older and a step ahead of Elias in the hierarchy, occupying the position of *Privatdozent*, an unpaid lecturer. Elias assisted Mannheim in his teaching, unofficially and unpaid. Heidelberg was a lively centre of the best in German sociology, Max Weber's influence was strong, and Elias 'spent a great deal of time reading Marx',[14] as well as Tönnies, Sombart, Troeltsch and Simmel.

There was, however, a fundamental opposition between Mannheim and Alfred Weber in which Elias took Mannheim's side and established one of the central themes of his approach to sociology from that point on, particularly his sociology of knowledge. In 1928, at the Sixth German Sociological Congress in Zurich, Mannheim gave a paper entitled 'Competition as a Cultural Phenomenon', in which he argued that ideas and knowledge develop largely through the dynamics of group competition. Weber complained that Mannheim appeared to be smuggling in a Marxist, materialist approach in disguise, and felt that Mannheim was going too far in seeing liberal political and ethical principles as socially constructed. What Weber missed in Mannheim's arguments was 'a recognition of intellectual creativity as a basis for action'.[15] Elias, however, spoke up on Mannheim's behalf, describing his paper as 'most decidedly revolutionary'.[16] Elias distanced himself from Weber's liberal humanism, saying:

> Whoever moves the 'creative human being' into the centre of his reflections retains the feeling of existing only for himself, constituting, as it were, a beginning and an end. But whoever moves the historical movements of human societies into the centre of his reflections must also know that he is neither beginning nor end, but rather a mere link in a chain.[17]

Like other critics, Elias came to feel that Mannheim, like Marx, had not said enough about how we could distinguish the validity or adequacy of knowledge, but he did agree that it was a mistake to ignore its social determination altogether. Later Elias wrote that his 'strongest feeling was of the enormous number of falsehoods that were spread around about human society',[18] usually presented as principles or ideas standing outside society and history, which was why 'Mannheim's central thesis that all thought is ideology was very congenial'[19] to him.

When Mannheim was offered a chair in Frankfurt after the publication of *Ideology and Utopia* in 1929, Mannheim agreed to supervise Elias immediately if he agreed to work as his assistant for three years. This was far more attractive than a four- to five-year wait with Weber, so in 1930 Elias moved to Frankfurt and a different set of intellectual influences.

FRANKFURT 1930–1933

Between 1930 and 1933 Elias worked as Mannheim's assistant, working in the same building as the *Institut für Psychoanalyse* and the *Institut für Sozialforschung*, the home of Max Horkheimer, Theodor Adorno, Erich Fromm, Friedrich Pollock, Leo Löwenthal and Herbert Marcuse, although there seems to have been little contact with the sociologists. Indeed, there was animosity between Mannheim and the *Institut* group, so Elias's association with Mannheim was an obstacle to such contact, although he seems to have been on good terms with Adorno. Mannheim only gave lectures, and Elias was responsible for the more direct contact with students, taking seminars and supervising dissertations.

We may never know what contact he had with Horkheimer, but Elias certainly took up many of the same concerns. In his inaugural lecture in 1931, Horkheimer stressed the importance of an interdisciplinary approach to social science, although he granted a more significant place to philosophy than Elias ever would, and he framed the future Institute's work in terms of the question of 'the connection between the economic life of society, the psychical development of individuals, and the changes in the realm of culture'.[20] The two had a similar sense of the importance of an analysis of psychic structure for social science; in 1932 Horkheimer commented on the lack of attention paid to psychology in sociology and history, arguing that since all societies are based on 'a definite development of human powers', they are all 'psychologically co-determined'. In analysing any historical epoch, then, 'it is especially important to know the psychic powers and dispositions, the character and mutability of the members of different social groups'.[21] In 1936, as Elias was putting the finishing touches to *Über den Prozeß der Zivilisation*, Horkheimer suggested that 'specific groups react according to the particular character of their members, which has been formed in the course of earlier as well as current social development', and that an understanding of both social stability and change requires 'a knowledge of the contemporary psychic make-up of people in various social groups, and in turn a knowledge of how their character has been formed in interaction with all the shaping cultural forces of the time'.[22]

Two of the Frankfurt students were Gisèle Freund and Ilse Seglow. Freund was an amateur photographer, so Elias encouraged her to pursue a dissertation on photography, and the two became friends. Freund took her thesis to the Sorbonne in 1933 and completed it in 1936. When Elias later wrote to Walter Benjamin, who also knew Freund, he began the letter with a reference to her. Similarly, he encouraged Ilse Seglow, who had worked as an actress, to make the theatre and the 'actor's society' the topic of her thesis. Seglow noted that she and other students regarded Elias as an excellent teacher, as well as commenting on his self-assurance: 'He seemed quite sure of what he wanted to do – too sure for some people's liking'.[23]

Elias was now part of a group of powerful intellects including Max Wertheimer the *Gestalt* psychologist, economist Adolf Löwe, philosopher Paul Tillich and psychoanalyst Sigmund Fuchs. Mannheim himself was a key figure, bringing with him from his contact with Georgy Lukács in Budapest all of the ideas of the 'cultural' turn in Western Marxism. Another vital element of the move from Heidelberg to Frankfurt was that recent psychological theory was taken far more seriously; the *Gestalt* psychologist Wertheimer was part of Mannheim's seminar, and later Elias said that 'probably Freud's ideas had a greater influence on my thinking than those of any theoretical sociologist'.[24] Although we should approach this assessment of the relative significance of other influences with caution, it is important to draw attention to the centrality of Freud's impact on Elias's thinking. Although Elias himself referred to the impact of Freud's *Civilization and its*

Discontents, of equal influence seems to have been *Future of an Illusion.*[25]

Three aspects of this book became threads running through all of Elias's work. First, Freud's opposition between instinctual pleasure and the requirements of social life; in his words: 'It seems . . . that every civilization must be built up on coercion and renunciation of instinct'.[26] Although Elias also argued that psychic structure was socially constituted, his persistent use of concepts like 'constraint' and 'restraint' prevented him forever properly escaping this basic Freudian (not to mention Hobbesian, or even Judeo-Christian) opposition between human nature and society. It was also to cause him considerable difficulty with critics in relation to his historicization of the idea, which we shall examine in Chapter 4. Second, the ideas contained in this passage:

> It is not true that the human mind has undergone no development since the earliest times and that, in contrast to the advances of science and technology, it is the same to-day as it was at the beginning of history. . . . It is in keeping with the course of human development that external coercion gradually becomes internalized; for a special mental agency, man's super-ego, takes it over and includes it among its commandments. Every child presents this process of transformation to us; only by that means does it become a moral and social being.[27]

Much of Elias's subsequent writing was an extension, elaboration and historical and sociological refinement of the points made by Freud here: the historical character of psychic life, the increasing internalization of external constraint, becoming internal constraint in the form of the superego, and the notion that the psychological development of children contains in 'reduced' form the basic elements of the broader historical transformation of the human psyche. This, too, would attract dispute from a number of critics.

Finally, Freud analysed the 'illusory' character of religious ideas, seeing them as 'fulfilments of the oldest, strongest and most urgent wishes of mankind',[28] particularly the desire to control that which lay beyond human control. Elias saw ample evidence of such illusions, or myths as he was to call them, in public life generally. He gained a particularly strong impression of the hold of emotionally charged mythology when – ever the curious empirical social scientist – he attended a Hitler rally disguised as an aristocrat, complete with monocle and 'a little hunter's hat'. But he also saw illusions and mythology at work among social scientists, and regarded the constant pursuit of what he called 'realistic' knowledge as the main aim of sociological thought. In one interview in 1984 he said that Mannheim's 'radical critique of ideologies appealed to my sense of how [many] phony ideas were around at the time'[29] and in another that 'I very sincerely think that we live in a forest of mythologies and that at the moment one of the main tasks is to clear it away'.[30] Throughout his life he thought along the lines of the conclusion to *The Future of an Illusion*: 'No, our science is no illusion. But illusion it would be to suppose that what science cannot give we can get elsewhere.'[31]

Die Höfische Mensch was completed early in 1933, but it was no longer of any practical consequence for Elias. The National Socialists were busy clearing out the left intellectuals from the universities, so Mannheim left for the London School of Economics and Political Science at Harold Laski's invitation. Elias stayed a little longer, until about March or April. A close friend, Grete Freudenthal, drove him to a number of cities in Switzerland – Basel, Zurich and Berne – looking for an academic post, without success. He returned to Breslau briefly to see his parents, and then moved on to Paris, again in pursuit of a university position.

PARIS/LONDON 1933–1953

He lived in Paris during the rest of 1933 and 1934, selling wooden toys for about nine months. He failed to get any academic position, with his connections in Paris at the Ecole Normal Supérieure, Alexander Koyre and sociologist Célestin Bouglé unable to find funds to employ him. Although Elias's French was good, it was not up to the level of fluency required for academic life, and being Jewish as well as a foreigner would have been an almost insurmountable barrier. Bouglé's influence was still significant, but not sufficient to overcome these obstacles.[32] Elias did, however, write his first two publications for German-language journals in 1935, 'Kitschstil im Kitschzeitalter' for *Die Sammlung* and 'Die Vertreibung der Hugenotten aus Frankreich' for *Der Ausweg*, and the second piece introduced a theme he would return to in the 1960s, the relationship between established and outsider groups. A friend from the Breslau and Heidelberg days, Alfred Glucksmann encouraged Elias, knowing little English, to move to London in 1935, although given his precarious financial situation he needed little persuasion.

For the next three years he worked exclusively on his next book project, which he hoped would enable him to obtain a position in England. Financial support came from a Dutch philanthropic foundation. It is unclear when he actually began on the work for this book; Elias himself suggests he began on his arrival in London, but in his preface he thanks Freund and Bouglé for their help, and both Detlev Schöttker and Stephen Mennell believe he must have started work on it earlier.[33] Both the Paris years and this period appear generally to have been quite happy for Elias. In Paris, although he was living from one day to the next, he was otherwise free of encumbrances. Once he was in London and had access to the library of the British Museum, he 'felt completely at home', more than content to spend every day reading, ordering books, taking notes and writing.

It is difficult to know exactly what the intellectual influences on Elias were while he was London, because he only ever referred to the ideas he encountered while in Germany. However, at the very least his footnotes indicate that the secondary sources he read included Johan Huizinga's *The Waning of the Middle Ages*,[34] Morris Ginsberg's *Sociology*,[35] William Ogburn's *Social Change*,[36] William Sumner's *Folkways*,[37] Charles Judd's *The Psychology of Social Institutions*,[38] Elsie Parsons' *Fear and Conventionality*,[39] and the collection of papers from the 1931 meeting of the American Sociological Society edited by Emory Bogardus, *Social Problems and Social Processes*.[40] All of these works provided a number of linkages into different intellectual traditions which fed into the conceptual apparatus of *Über den Prozeß der Zivilisation* and formed an additional layer of influence over his previous theoretical development in Germany.

Elias wrote that the 'more general problem' which he was addressing 'has also been posed for a long time by American sociology',[41] mentioning Sumner's *Folkways*. He cited Sumner's remarks about the necessity of examining exactly what any given culture's morals, norms and values were and how they arose, adding that it was also important to apply the analysis to 'our own society and its history'. Parsons' book also drew his attention to Franz Boas's work and William James's conception of 'habit' as 'the enormous flywheel of society'.[42]

Elias had come across the notion of the 'unintended consequences of human action' before, in Hegel's 'cunning of reason', and in Marx, both of whom had read Adam Smith. But it was Sumner's *Folkways* which seems to have provided the most thought-through linkage of Elias's interests in culture and behaviour with the concept's original formulation in Adam Ferguson and the other Scottish Enlightenment theorists. Sumner wrote:

> From recurrent needs arise habits for the individual and customs for the group, but these results are consequences

which were never conscious, and never foreseen or intended. . . . Another long time must pass, and a higher stage of mental development must be reached, before they can be used as a basis from which to deduce rules for meeting, in the future, problems whose pressure can be foreseen. The folkways, therefore, are not creations of human purpose and wit . . . all the life of human beings, in all ages and stages of culture, is primarily controlled by a vast mass of folkways handed down from the earliest existence of the race, only the topmost layers of which are subject to change and control, and have been somewhat modified by human philosophy, ethics, and religion, or by other acts of intelligent reflection.[43]

'Folkways' was a different way of talking about 'civilization', and Sumner's ideas on their unplanned nature and historicity at least resonated with Elias's ideas if they did not help generate them. They reinforced Elias's critique of the notion of 'sovereign' power, and his conception of the unplanned nature of historical change.

Sumner could only contrast 'civilized' to 'primitive' folkways, but there was a more precise historical understanding of forms of behaviour and social interaction in Huizinga's *The Waning of the Middle Ages*, providing Elias with a detailed picture of everyday life in the Middle Ages which he could contrast with the contemporary world. As Johan Goudsblom has pointed out, the brevity of Elias's references to Huizinga mask the significance of his influence. Huizinga drew his attention to the writings of Erasmus as well as the type of historical material which would be used to demonstrate the historical character of human psychology, and sensitized him to the significance of manners and etiquette as expressions of both people's psychic lives and the structure of their social relations.[44] The opening chapter of *The Waning of the Middle Ages* was titled 'The violent tenor of life',[45] and Huizinga wrote of Europe five centuries earlier:

The contrast between suffering and joy, between adversity and happiness, appeared more striking. All experience had yet to the minds of men the directness and absoluteness of the pleasure and pain of child-life. Every event, every action, was still embodied in expressive and solemn forms, which raised them to the dignity of a ritual . . . all things presented themselves to the mind in violent contrasts and impressive forms, lent a tone of excitement and of passion to everyday life and tended to produce that perpetual oscillation between despair and distracted joy, between cruelty and pious tenderness which characterize life in the Middle Ages.[46]

Huizinga's picture of medieval life, especially its ferocity, insecurity and emotionality made a powerful impression on Elias, and a very similar understanding of the contrast between medieval and modern social life runs through the whole of *The Civilizing Process*. Indeed, Elias's work is best understood when it is read alongside Huizinga's book.

Charles Judd, Professor of Education at the University of Chicago, also added to the argument Elias had encountered in Freud's *Civilization and its Discontents* and *Future of an Illusion*, of the social and historical character of human psychology, alerting him at the same time to the fact that this was a minority position in mainstream psychology. 'Emphasis on the social forces which operate to determine the course of human development', wrote Judd, 'has not been common in treatises on psychology',[47] and he added that even when social elements are considered, they are treated as the products of 'so-called instincts such as gregariousness, communicativeness, and gang spirit . . . [which] . . . are described as personal traits which all men bring into the world through inheritance and out of which in some mysterious fashion spring nations and languages and codes of morals'.[48] Elias's line of argument in *Über den Prozeß der Zivilisation* had strong parallels with Judd's suggestion that the historical development of a variety of social institutions has not merely been accompanied by different forms of behaviour, but 'it has also affected emotions to such an extent that we are entirely justified in saying that civilized man has an emotional equipment which is widely different from that of primitive man and the animals',[49] although Elias clearly rejected the linkage between 'primitive man' and animals.

Judd also drew Elias's attention to the importance of a particular regulation of *time* in the establishment of complex social forms and the behaviour they demand of individuals. 'The impressive fact about the modern method of life,' wrote Judd, 'is that it finally takes so firm a hold on the individual that he becomes a living embodiment of the social demand that everyone guide his conduct by the clock . . . which reaches into the individual nervous system and dominates the behaviour and thinking of each and every member of society'.[50] However, apart from the brief mention in *Über den Prozeß der Zivilisation*, it took over forty years before Elias returned to this theme in his essay on time.[51]

Bogardus's collection of papers on the concept of social process was essentially a survey of the treatment of the concept 'social process' by a wide variety of American sociologists to date, and it drew Elias's attention to the work of Albion Small, Charles Ellwood, George Herbert Mead, Howard Becker, Charles Cooley, as well as Florian Znaniecki, Pitirim Sorokin and Robert MacIver, whose conference papers were in the volume. So enamoured were this generation of American sociologists with the concept 'social process', that one contributor, Read Bain, felt obliged to sound a note of warning that it was being used too loosely and too broadly, thus emptying it of its explanatory value and becoming another example of 'pseudo-scientific jargon'.[52]

There would have been much about this book that Elias would have found confused and inadequate, but there were some lines of argument that he was sympathetic to. Approaching social life in terms of processes *at all* was important for Elias, and most of these writers had an interest in trying to analyse long-term processes of social change without lapsing into normative and teleological conceptions of evolution and progress. Robert MacIver, for example, argued that it was important to look for the formative processes which lie behind any given social pattern:

> Beyond the fabric there is not only the loom and the weaver but also the weaving. Beyond the social pattern there is the play of forces emanating from the endless interaction of group and environment. By studying the fabric alone we could never understand the process of weaving, and we will never come to grips with the problem of social causation by studying its contemporary resultant patterns.[53]

In order to explain social life, MacIver felt, it was necessary to 'study society genetically'. This was self-evident to nineteenth-century European sociologists, of course, but little of their work had been translated, and to the Americans it was still an important argument. MacIver argued, in terms which were to be echoed in the 1970s and 1980s, that 'the time-dimension is seriously lacking in our sociological studies today, and our presentation of social change is apt to be merely a series of successive pictures as lacking in the dynamic of real life as those we see upon the screen',[54] although today we may disagree about the realism of the screen! More significantly, it was this book and this discussion in American sociology, building on the ideas of Small and Cooley, which drew Elias's attention to the concept of 'process', and gave him a vitally important conceptual reference point around which he could organize his thoughts about the development of European civilization.

Morris Ginsberg was the leading sociologist in Britain, challenged only by Mannheim's joining him at the London School of Economics and Political Science (LSE). In Ginsberg's book Elias would have found support for his relational view of human social life (Ginsberg spoke frequently of society as networks of social relations), the 'plasticity' of psychic and emotional life and the unintentional nature of social change. What counts in analysing society, argued Ginsberg, was less individual actions than the 'way they are corrected, modified, and adapted to each other in the final result. In this way slight changes in individuals may sum up to something of the greatest significance in the whole, and common actions may have consequences which are never willed or foreseen by those who took part in them'.[55] Ginsberg, like Ogburn, also supported the notion of *directional* but not teleological historical development:

> It is important to remember, at the outset, that when we speak of trends of developments we must not think of them as occurring inevitably or automatically. We can point to no order of ideas or social institution whose growth can be traced through a regular sequence of stages repeated in the same order among different peoples. The most that we can hope to do is to indicate a movement in humanity as a whole, which, despite actions and reactions, reveals some persistent direction.[56]

Elias would produce similar formulations throughout his lifetime. Ginsberg also spoke of 'the process of civilization',[57] and he concluded his book with a reference to the possibility that human beings might become able to control their own destinies. Examining the notion of a 'self-directed humanity', its theoretical implications, and 'the possibilities of its realization', may be said to be the ultimate object of sociology.[58] Again, Elias saw the potential contribution to be made by sociologists in an almost identical light.

In a letter to Goudsblom he once suggested he had only a slight familiarity with sociological literature at this time. He wrote:

> my ability to write *Über den Prozeß der Zivilisation* was to some extent due to the fact that my knowledge of the books which are now declared the standard books of a sociologists' ancestors was at the time of writing this book extremely deficient.[59]

He often criticized philosophers for creating the impression that science 'springs from the head of man fully antecedent and fully armed like Athene from the head of Zeus',[60] but he displayed precisely this tendency in his concern to avoid discussion of his own antecedents and sources of inspiration. Indeed, his self-assessment suggests that to a large extent he actively sought the position of a sociological maverick, an outsider. As an account of his intellectual background it is wholly inaccurate, as he himself said later in his autobiographical notes, commenting that he never saw himself 'as marking a beginning, an innovator starting from nothing. . . . I was highly conscious of myself as a man of my generations.'[61] In the Heidelberg and Frankfurt days he had absorbed almost all of the best in German sociology, if not by reading Marx, Weber, Simmel, Troeltsch and Tönnies, then in discussion with a group of sophisticated intellectuals who had. In Paris he probably gained at least an impression of Durkheimian sociology in discussions with Celestin Bouglé. In London, this body of ideas was to join forces with those of Ginsberg and American sociologists such as Sumner, Ogburn, and, indirectly, Small, Cooley and Mead, as well as the intellectual traditions – particularly the Scottish Enlightenment theorists – they drew upon. In general we can say that Elias was well-acquainted, either directly or indirectly with, if not the entire field of European, English and American sociological thought, then certainly the most important ideas that sociologists had produced up to the 1930s, as well as with Freud and the *Gestalt* psychologists.[62]

Armed, then, with a sophisticated conceptual apparatus, Elias set to work on his book. Every day he would go to the British Museum Library, ordering books whenever footnotes attracted his attention, initially with the intention of writing about French liberalism. However, he stumbled across a variety of editions of books on etiquette, which resonated with the work he had already done on social interaction in French court society. They provided powerful empirical illustration of Freud's comment on the historical nature of human character, a theme which Karl Mannheim was also interested in. Later Elias said that he saw his work on *Über den Prozeß der Zivilisation* as a critique of the bulk of academic psychology, where it was assumed that one could only analyse human psychology in terms of real human beings who could be measured or assessed in a direct way,[63] whereas he was undertaking a historical analysis of the development of human personality structure.

The first volume was completed around late 1936 and the second at the end of 1938. In April 1938 he was invited by philosopher Anders Karitz to contribute to a lecture series at the University of Uppsala, and he spent six weeks in Sweden, apparently in the hope of finding a position there. His paper outlined many of the book's major themes, although it was only published much later as part of *The Society of Individuals*, – in German in 1987, and in English in 1991. It proved very difficult to get the book into print because of the situation in Germany. The first publisher disappeared, and his father had difficulty getting hold of the money to pay for another. Eventually it was published by a German exile publisher, Fritz Karger. However, it was not a good time for German books, and when Elias visited his publisher after the war, more copies had been sent for review than had been sold, and he said to Elias: 'Look, it's filling up my cellar. Couldn't we pulp it? No one wants to buy it.'[64] Reviews appeared in *The Sociological Review* by Franz Borkeneau, an acquaintance from the Frankfurt days, and *Les Annales Sociologiques* by Raymond Aron, who had met Elias while visiting Mannheim in Frankfurt in 1932,[65] as well as in number of Dutch journals.[66]

The reviewer Elias had in mind for the readership among German intellectuals in exile was Walter Benjamin, also a friend of Gisela Freund's, and the journal he hoped the review would appear in was the Frankfurt Institute's *Zeitschrift für Sozialforschung*. In his letter to Benjamin,[67] Elias mentions Erich Fromm as another potential reviewer, but Fromm had become more sceptical about psychoanalysis, and seemed less appropriate than Benjamin, who was still asserting the importance of an integration of Marxism and psychoanalysis. However, Benjamin was both understandably preoccupied with his own situation as a German Jew in Paris in 1938, and not very responsive to the first volume. Elias wrote to him again, explaining that the purpose of the book was to use his historical material to develop a theoretical understanding of the development of psychic structures, but Benjamin regarded it as primarily cultural history and suggested he look for another reviewer. Above all, Benjamin objected to the absence of a prioritization of class analysis: 'what one is to understand as social psychology is,' felt Benjamin, 'to be determined first on the basis of a social theory which has made its primary theme the opposition between classes'.[68]

There was a dark side to this extremely productive period in Elias's life, however. His parents visited him in 1938, and he did his best to persuade them to stay in England, but such a move was too dramatic for an elderly couple, and they returned to Breslau, convinced that no harm would come to them because they had done no wrong. In 1940, he heard from Sophie that his father had died, not long after having exerted all his efforts to publish Elias's book, and Sophie herself disappeared shortly after to Auschwitz, where she died, Elias assumed in 1941. The forty-four-year-old Elias was understandably badly affected by this; he said later that he felt guilty for failing to persuade them to stay in London, and the image of his mother in a concentration camp haunted him. 'I still remember very clearly. . . . Of course, I shall never get over it. I'll never get over it.'[69] It seems likely that his own reluctance about making *Über den Prozeß der Zivilisation* more easily available and having it translated into English – it took forty years – as well as the difficulties he encountered writing to the same level of productivity, were related to the associations between his book and these tragic events.

On publishing *Über den Prozeß der Zivilisation*, he gained a

Senior Research Fellowship at the LSE. The LSE was evacuated to Cambridge, where he spent a few months, but not long afterwards he was interned on the Isle of Man as an enemy alien for eight months. C.P. Snow and Morris Ginsberg helped extract him, and he returned briefly to Cambridge where he continued his friendship with Snow and Glucksmann. But there was no work, and he returned to London, where there was only a little more. Barbara Wootton and Morris Ginsberg helped him with occasional lectures and teaching, but for some reason Mannheim, who had moved to a chair in the Sociology of Education at the University of London, was unable or unwilling to provide any assistance.

The next decade was a bleak period. He wrote an article for the first volume of the *British Journal of Sociology* entitled 'Studies in the genesis of the naval profession', which drew upon a point made in *Über den Prozeß der Zivilisation* about the relationship between navies and armies. Elias co-founded a Group Analysis society with Foulkes[70] and others, and went into psychoanalysis himself. When asked why, he said it was because he wrote so slowly, although he also wrote to Cas Wouters that the analysis helped him get beyond 'an ineradicable guilt feeling that I was unable to get my mother out of the concentration camp before she died in a gas chamber'.[71] Elias had his fair share of Holocaust trauma, guilt and reparation to deal with. While most sociologists of comparative age were at the peak of their productivity, in established academic positions, on journal editorial boards, gathering postgraduate students and like-minded scholars and developing their scholarly reputations, Elias was surviving on part-time teaching and adult education.

His luck turned in 1954 when, at the age of fifty-seven, he was offered lectureships by Ilya Neustadt at Leicester and Eugene Grebenick at Leeds, choosing Leicester because of its closer proximity to London. He was not keen to leave London and the British Museum library, but it was a full-time position, and 'Leicester was a pretty, clean, medium-sized city, and had the additional advantage that one could travel to London and back in a day'.[72]

LEICESTER/GHANA 1954–1974

Leicester was still a very small institution, a college affiliated to the University of London, but sociology was to grow significantly in England during the 1950s and 1960s, and the Leicester department played a central role in the formation of English sociology. Between 1954 and 1957 Elias and Neustadt were on their own, teaching the sociology program as part of the University of London Economics degree taught externally at Leicester. John Goldthorpe joined them in 1957, the year that Leicester was granted full University status, followed by Richard Brown and others in 1959. By the mid-1960s, as Richard Brown recollects, Neustadt and Elias were in charge of 'probably the largest honours school in sociology in the country with some sixty students graduating each year'.[73] Elias had particular responsibility for the first-year course, and a number of now-prominent English intellectuals either studied at Leicester or worked alongside Elias. The list includes Martin Albrow, Sheila Allen, Joe and Olive Banks, Richard Brown, Chris Bryant, Percy Cohen, John Eldridge, Eric Dunning, Anthony Giddens, John H. Goldthorpe, Paul Hirst, Keith Hopkins, Mary McIntosh, Nicos Mouzelis, Graeme Salaman and Bryan Wilson. Martin Albrow recalls finding himself, together with Giddens and Hopkins, at the back of Elias's Introduction to Sociology lectures, 'not altogether willingly, constrained by his insistence (rightly) that new lecturers in their mid-twenties had an awful lot to learn'.[74]

The lectures included a rich variety of material on social conditions throughout the world, based on United Nations figures, giving students both a comparative perspective on world society and a historical sense of the developments in social conditions over longer periods of time. As Johan Goudsblom points out, most students and co-lecturers did not experience this approach as particular to Elias, but regarded it as self-evident, absorbing it into the background of their own sociological orientation, often

without a clear sense of which ideas arose from a shared sociological tradition and which were Elias's own contributions. 'His
younger colleagues,' writes Goudsblom, 'were generally full of
admiration for the leading figures of American sociology, but
regarded Elias's own ideas as the somewhat eccentric views of an
old-fashioned continental European'.[75] Goudsblom recalls meeting him at an International Sociological Association conference
in 1956, and how the American sociologists suddenly decided
it was time for a cup of coffee when it came to Elias's turn to
speak. It was primarily in the Netherlands, where more social
scientists could read German, that *Über den Prozeß der Zivilisation*
was exerting an influence among scholars such as Goudsblom,
Anton Blok and Godfried van Benthem van den Bergh. The
extent of Elias's isolation was indicated when he confided to
Renate Rubinstein, years after the event, that when Goudsblom
asked to be introduced to him at the 1956 ISA conference, he was
surprised because it was the first time anyone had made such a
request. Indeed, it was the first time he had encountered anyone
outside his personal network who had read *Über den Prozeß der
Zivilisation.*[76]

In his writing he returned to one of the interests of his younger
days, the sociology of knowledge, publishing 'Problems of involvement and detachment' in the *British Journal of Sociology* in 1956.
The more central conceptual concerns of *Über den Prozeß der
Zivilisation* only began to re-emerge gradually in his contribution
to the reworking of a thesis by John L. Scotson, *The Established
and the Outsiders*, published in 1965, where he also developed
the ideas first raised in one of his Paris publications. He also wrote
a piece on the use of personal pronouns as a conceptual tool,
parts of which were to be published much later in *The Society
of Individuals.*[77] He gave the paper in front of his colleagues at
Leicester, and recalled that 'it was not at all well received. . . . The
young people in the department probably regarded my innovative
ideas as continental whimsy . . . they did oppose me violently.'[78]

Elias's confident self-assuredness about the innovatory nature of his sociological ideas and his disdain for engaging with current theoretical debates grated on most of his English colleagues. Nicos Mouzelis, for example, regards his isolation as 'self-inflicted', and remarks sharply on 'his unwillingness to consider *seriously* anybody's else's work, including work directly related to his major concerns'.[79]

The dominant ethos in sociology, since the 1950s at least, has been to develop one's sociological position *through* a debate with key early and contemporary sociologists and philosophers, whereas Elias regarded the discussion of other writers largely as a distraction, usually relegating comments on his sources and related research to his footnotes. He thought and wrote as many of the later nineteenth- and early twentieth-century scholars – Weber, Simmel, Mannheim, Freud – did, minimizing his engagement with other thinkers and focusing on a direct engagement with his topic. In many respects this was a wise choice, because commentary on other writers was not his strong point. When he did attempt direct theoretical criticism, he was often accused of caricature.[80] His theoretical talents lay in a different direction, in absorbing the essence of what was useful and productive in writers he read, integrating their insights with other ideas and utilizing the resultant synthesis of concepts in the analysis of a specific body of evidence. However, this ran so strongly counter to the disciplinary orientation of sociologists in the post-war decades that, as he put it, 'Whenever I brought out an unusual idea in one of my annual lectures for my colleagues, it resulted in a very hostile argument with the younger generation'.[81] His English colleagues treated him with 'a lightly condescending affection',[82] but only occasionally with intellectual respect.

Elias also wrote a piece on the Eichmann trial in 1961–62, entitled 'The breakdown of civilization', which explored the implications of National Socialism for our understanding of 'civilization'. It was not published, however, until 1987 in German and

1996 in English, as part of *The Germans*, which was unfortunate given that many of his critics thought that a major weakness of his approach was the lack of attention paid to such recent examples of 'civilized barbarism'.

When he retired at the age of sixty-five, the offer of a chair turned up in Ghana, so, ever-interested in adventure, he left England for Africa in 1962. In the two years he spent there he did some fieldwork with his students, but it has never been written up. He also gathered impressions of African culture and social life which he later, in the 1970s and 1980s, referred to in discussions with interviewers of his understanding of civilizing processes. He took the intellectually risky step of reiterating a comparison he had made in *Über den Prozeß der Zivilisation* between African and medieval society, attracting considerable and heated criticism from anthropologists, indeed from most scholars interested in cross-cultural analysis. Anton Blok, for example, who had made extensive use of Elias's ideas in his own work, found this too much to bear and parted ways with the notion of 'civilization' at a conference in the Netherlands in 1981. Blok argued that it had become clear that the concept 'civilization' was far too weighed down with the accompanying baggage of an opposition to the 'primitive'; consequently, it could not be used as a social-scientific concept and escape the connotations of its more common-sense meaning of 'superior' and 'Western'.

In 1964 he returned to Leicester, with annual renewals of his teaching contract, and from this point onwards he returned to his pre-war levels of productivity. During this period he began to co-operate with Eric Dunning in writing on the sociology of sport. Dunning and Elias agreed that sport was an important example of the regulation and management of emotions, playing a significant role in everyday life in modern societies. He wrote a piece on nationalism, but it was only published later in *The Germans*. In 1969 *Über den Prozeß der Zivilisation* was re-published in German, along with *Die Höfische Gesellschaft* with a new introduction. His article on 'Sociology and psychiatry'[83] picked up his interest in the sociological understanding of psychology and individual experience. *Was ist Soziologie?* appeared in 1970, outlining in a more formal, textbook-style way Elias's sociological approach. In the 1970s he intensified his discussion of the sociology of knowledge and science, publishing a two-part article in *Sociology*,[84] another in *Economy & Society*,[85] and a chapter in a collection on the sociology of science edited by Richard Whitley.[86] In 1973 *Über den Prozeß der Zivilisation* was translated into French and began selling well. In Germany, students discovered the 1969 re-issue of *Über den Prozeß der Zivilisation*, and read it alongside Foucault's book *Discipline and Punish* as an account of the increasingly disciplined character of modern social life.

AMSTERDAM 1975–1978

Elias's intellectual reputation was growing slowly, not in England where he had been teaching, but in Germany, the Netherlands and France. German and Dutch sociologists and historians had been inviting him to guest posts since 1969, in Amsterdam (1969/1970), the Hague (1971), Bielefeld, Konstanz, Aachen (1975/1976) and Bochum. In 1976 a paperback edition of *Über den Prozeß der Zivilisation* appeared in German, and in 1977 he was awarded the Theodor Adorno prize by the city of Frankfurt, and the University of Frankfurt made him an Emeritus Professor. The first volume of *Über den Prozeß der Zivilisation* was translated into English in 1978, published by a German/American publisher, and the second in 1982. This separation in the publication dates was to be a source of constant confusion in the English-language interpretations of *The Civilizing Process*, with reviewers responding primarily to the first volume without taking into account the arguments in the second. The reviews indicating a real understanding of Elias's project came from those who, like Martin Albrow,[87] were able to read both volumes of the German edition.

In the Netherlands he was developing a following among Dutch sociologists and historians, centred on the University of Amsterdam. In 1970, for example, Nico Wilterdink wrote, under an alias, a satirical piece for the student newspaper on the almost religious atmosphere of admiration and awe which had come to surround Elias:

> In the Sociology Institute and the History Seminar, little else is talked about apart from Elias, Elias and Elias. That is quite understandable, because Elias is a godsend. He is a godsend for disillusioned social scientists who have lost their faith in American social science, but not their faith in the social sciences as such, and who shudder at Marxist or Marcusian hocus-pocus. And now there is finally someone who not only proclaims with great vigour what they actually long thought, but who also manages to fill the vacuum of doubt and scepticism with something entirely new.[88]

Goudsblom's conviction that Elias's approach to sociology transcended many of the conflicts and disputes in contemporary sociology was clearly articulated in his *Sociology in the Balance*,[89] and as senior Professor of Sociology at Amsterdam his view carried weight. There was also considerable criticism, but in the long run this heightened the interest in Elias and made it even more interesting and important to read him. Much the same dynamic can be seen in relation to any writer – most recently, Foucault, Derrida, Baudrillard, Giddens – where the right mixture of criticism and admiration significantly expands their readership.

BIELEFELD 1978–1984

By this time he was spending so much more time in Germany and the Netherlands, giving guest lectures and seminars, that he left his house in Leicester in 1978. Between 1978 and 1984 he lived and worked at the Zentrum für Interdisziplinäre Forschung (ZiF) in Bielefeld, extremely productive despite failing eyesight. Now in his eighties, he had a strong sense of the limited time left to him and he continued to feel that his work had not yet been properly understood, and that he still had much to say and write. He worked with the help of a number of assistants, usually post-graduate sociology students, gave frequent guest lectures as well as numerous radio and television interviews, and in 1980 the University of Bielefeld awarded him an honorary doctorate.

It was in this period that he worked on the German editions of books such as *The Society of Individuals* and *Involvement and Detachment* which combined earlier work with his more recent ideas, wrote *The Loneliness of the Dying* (later translated into French by Michel Foucault, although Foucault's translation was never published), continued his work on the sociology of science in journal articles and book chapters, and wrote a paper on the formation of German national identity for the German Sociology Congress in 1980 which was later taken up in *The Germans*.

The increasing attention being paid to Elias's work, both admiring and critical, brought with it new influences on the formation and, perhaps more importantly, the re-formation of his ideas. Commentators often stress the continuity of Elias's thinking, but it is equally important to be aware of how his ideas developed in response to criticism, discussion and current debates. When his arguments were described in terms he felt were too simplistic or inaccurate, he was moved to formulate the relevant ideas differently. When critics attacked, for instance, his argument about the increasingly balanced management of violence with the obvious example of the Holocaust, it provided an added impetus towards analysing the twentieth-century development of German society, although he had already started giving thought to this question in the 1960s. This line of thought also led him to change his position on the overall direction of civilizing processes, placing greater emphasis on the possibility of '*de*civilizing processes', and to explore in more detail the specific, distinctive developments of society, culture and habitus in particular countries. He was also sensitive to the overall political context of world society in the 1970s and 1980s, placing greater emphasis on the potential for violence between states than he had in his earlier work, where there was more of a focus on interpersonal violence and its trans-formations.

BACK TO AMSTERDAM 1985–1990

From 1985 onwards he remained in Amsterdam, writing his books on *Time, The Symbol Theory* and his autobiography. In 1985 he was invited by Pierre Bourdieu, who had been impressed by his work on the sociology of sport in the 1970s, to give lectures at the Collège de France and the Ecole des Hautes Etudes en Sciences Sociales. The ethnologist Hans-Peter Duerr also began writing his multi-volume critique of Elias's work, *The Myth of the Civilizing Process*,[90] to which Elias responded in 1988, along with a variety of other commentators.

In 1988, he received the Premio Europeo Amalfi prize for *Die Gesellschaft der Individuen* (The Society of Individuals) as the best sociology book published in Europe in 1987, and in 1989 the Italian Nonio Prize, travelling to Udine, his health failing, to receive the prize. Shortly after a fall produced a lung infection, and he died in his chair on a hot afternoon on 1 August 1990.

Elias laid great stress in his writings on the importance of intellectual detachment and the destructive impact of emotional, ideologically founded involvement on our ability to deal effec-tively with important human problems. We shall examine this aspect of his approach to sociology in Chapter 5. In practical terms he was detached from the political life around him, and a major difference with Karl Mannheim was his more pessimistic estimation of the likely immediate effectiveness of a utilization of sociological knowledge in the political arena. His Dutch inter-viewers in 1984 were clearly frustrated by his refusal to explore *how* his ideas might have had any real effect in the world around him, remaining content with committing his insights to paper or talking about them to whoever would listen in his circle of students, colleagues and friends.[91] This was about as close as Elias got to a theology, his faith in the written word and the power of personal persuasion.

What can easily be overlooked, however, is how passionate an intellectual he actually was. He channelled all his energy and commitment into his research and teaching, including that which many of us put into partners and children. He wrote in a letter to Wouters:

> it is necessary for every grown up person – necessary for a person's own mental health, to find a balance between the pre-occupation with his or her own immediate needs for warmth and love and sexual gratification, for companionship and friendship on the one hand and, on the other hand, the devotion to a solid task of a less personal nature, a task for others without which no sense of personal fulfilment is possible.[92]

Although he strove for intellectual detachment, regarding self-discipline as the most secure foundation for an effective management of the problems of human existence, he did so in an extremely 'involved' way, pouring almost all of his life and soul into what he hoped would eventually become the very *political* task of analysing society. It is in this sense that he was one of the few truly 'public intellectuals' who, in being both admired and criticized, makes a real contribution to the enrichment of human social life.

3

TOWARDS A THEORY OF HUMAN SOCIETY

Elias was never concerned to spend much effort criticizing or commenting on, let alone outlining or reconstructing, other theorists' ideas. He devoted detailed critical attention to only a handful of writers, including Karl Marx, August Comte, Talcott Parsons and Karl Popper, but he tended to treat them as exemplifying dominant trends in contemporary social science, rather than aiming to make any contribution to a better or different understanding of their work. Other comments on theorists such as Weber, Freud and Mannheim were made only in passing, and often they have been regarded as superficial, sometimes erroneous. His understanding of Weber's concept of 'ideal types', for example, is best regarded as problematic. When he was being critical of other sociological approaches, he frequently preferred to keep his critique implicit, so that only a careful 'reading between the lines' could unearth the positions he was distancing himself from. He tended to speak in a very vague and global way of 'sociologists today', 'philosophy', or 'historians', rather than specifying particular authors or positions, and hardly ever indicated where other social scientists might have been pursuing similar lines of argument. It was far more important for him to engage in the empirical investigation of particular research problems. This has often given the impression that he was not a strong theorist – some have suggested a weak one – with his primary strength lying in his empirical historical studies.

However, this is only true to the extent that we restrict our conception of 'theory' to the discussion of other writers. The fact that he had little to say about other sociologists, or that we may have reason to be critical of what he did say about them, does not mean that he was not developing a powerful and intricate theoretical position. In fact, his work constitutes a complex theoretical system, and this applies to the conceptual arguments which run through studies like *The Civilizing Process* as well as to the more explicitly theoretical works like *The Society of Individuals* and *What is Sociology?* His theory tended to be embedded within his sociological *practice*, in his method of doing sociology, rather than being self-consciously presented as such.

He refrained from making the claim that he was developing a 'theoretical system' because he wanted to avoid the tendency towards fetishizing theory, theorists and theoretical perspectives, at the expense of getting on with the practice of sociological investigation. Elias preferred simply to develop his conceptual framework in the process of conducting his research, and thus overcome the divide between theory and research which still plagues sociology. But it was, nonetheless, an ambitious theoretical system. As he put it, he saw his task as one of drawing on the work of Marx, Weber and Freud, *inter alia*, and 'elaborating a comprehensive theory of human society, or, more exactly, a theory of the development of humanity, which could provide an integrating framework of reference for the various specialist social sciences'.[1] All of the conceptual arguments he engaged in throughout his writings are part of this 'comprehensive theory', each of them interlinked with the others.

In the process, Elias was also concerned to develop a different form of *perception* of the social world.[2] He believed that many of the problems and obstacles in contemporary social science were built into the very categories and concepts around which thought about society and human behaviour was organized. His work consists in large measure of an argument for a particular sociological vocabulary and conceptual framework, which in turn has embedded within it a form of social perception he believed would get closer to the reality of human social life. A number of concepts are important here: figuration, process, habitus, civilization, relation, network/web, power-ratio, interdependence, established/outsiders, involvement/detachment, not only in themselves, but also as radical alternatives to the standard concepts used by most sociologists in the second half of the twentieth century: society, system, structure, role, action, interaction, individual, reproduction. He was, however, always aware of how *problematic* an exercise this was, that most concepts which made sense both to himself and his readers could only partially capture the reality he wanted to talk about. This in turn contributed to his hesitancy about proclaiming his work as *the* theoretical position around which we all had to rally. He was conscious of the essentially *provisional* and *partial* character of all of his concepts, the validity of which would always be contingent on the way they made sense of any given body of empirical evidence.[3]

Although he was willing to present his sociological theory for some time as organized around the concept of 'figuration', he grew to dislike the term 'figurational sociology' and ended up preferring 'process sociology' as a label. It should be said, however, that even this was insufficient, in that he was not adopting a pluralist position, arguing for one approach among many, but for how all sociology should be approached, and in this sense even 'process sociology' is inadequate to the extent that it suggests that it is possible to pursue a *non*-process sociology.

BEYOND THE STRUCTURE/AGENCY DICHOTOMY

By way of an introduction to Elias's theoretical position, it is useful to refer briefly to the one sociological theorist he did discuss at any length – Talcott Parsons. When they met in 1970 at the ISA conference in Varna, Elias praised his integrity, sincerity and his power of theoretical synthesis, but added: 'I cannot persuade myself that this gift has been used in the right cause.'[4] Elias made essentially two points about Parsons and, through them, sociology more broadly.

The first was the organization of sociological thought around the concept of 'action'. 'Why put "actions" in the centre of a theory of society,' said Elias, 'and not the people who act? If anything, societies are networks of human beings in the round, not a medley of disembodied actions.'[5] Parsons' theory of action was rooted in his formulation of what he called the 'Hobbesian problem of order', namely, the apparent problem of how we can explain the orderliness of human society given that every individual pursues his or her own independent ends. Parsons embarked on an argument against what he saw as the utilitarian position, that only external constraint could produce such order, putting forward the supposedly more sociological view that order emerged from the internalization of social norms, what came to be established in sociology as the concept of 'socialization'. The basic problem here is that Parsons, like the writers he argues against, assumed that social orderliness is *external* to human individuals. His argument was only about *how* that external constraint should be conceptualized, in terms of brute force or norms and socialization.[6]

The division of sociological thought into what Alan Dawe called 'the two sociologies',[7] those of structure and those of action, emerges from interaction between this position and a continued attachment to individualist liberal ideals of autonomy and freedom. Attempts to oppose the determinism of structuralist approaches with action theories merely approach the dualism from a different angle, proposing that social order can emerge from autonomous individuals emancipated from external constraint. As Elias put it, 'one of the strongest motive forces of people who insist on starting their theoretical reflections about societies from "individuals *per se*" or from "individual acts" seems to be the wish to assert that "basically" an individual is "free"'.[8] Randall Collins argues similarly in this regard, that the 'longing for agency' is a retreat to 'a subjective world constructed so as to offer the fantasy of subjective power'.[9] Apparent attempts to transcend the agency/structure division, such as Anthony Giddens' 'structuration theory', merely reproduce it and pose it in a different form because of the continued conceptual opposition of 'action' to 'structure'; as Collins puts it, 'the result looks curiously like the Parsonian scheme that Giddens criticizes'.[10]

To the extent that Parsons' understanding of human action as organized around the linking of means and ends has been followed within sociology, with the only argument being about how the ends are determined, sociologists have forgotten an essential feature of the classical sociologists' understanding of human behaviour which Elias retained, namely, their emphasis on the importance of particular *psychological* formations of individuals in explaining social life. Charles Camic points out that an important concept which the early sociologists organized much of their work around was 'habit', 'habitus', 'habitude', a concept which Parsons 'wrote out of the whole history of modern social theory',[11] and which few writers have written back into it. The exceptions have included Wilhelm Reich, the Frankfurt School theorists – Horkheimer, Adorno, Marcuse, and the early Fromm – and more recently, Elias, Camic, Pierre Bourdieu and, to a lesser extent, Randall Collins. However, as R.W. Connell points out, 'There have been no effective successors to this generation of theorists. Historical depth psychology remains a gleam in the theoretical eye rather than an established branch of knowledge.'[12]

The concept of habit or *habitus* refers to 'the durable and generalized disposition that suffuses a person's action throughout an entire domain of life or, in the extreme instance, throughout all of life – in which case the term comes to mean the whole manner, turn, cast, or mold of the personality'.[13] Elias called it 'second nature'. As Durkheim wrote, anticipating Freud, 'it is not enough to direct our attention to the superficial portion of our consciousness; for the sentiments, the ideas which come to the surface are not, by far, those which have the most influence on our conduct. What must be reached are the habits . . . these are the real forces which govern us.'[14] Weber's work on the 'spirit of capitalism' showed a similar concern with habit, not just in relation to traditional action, but also modern instrumentally rational action, which Weber felt also rested on a foundation of habit. His concept of the 'capitalist spirit' referred to 'the development of [a] particular *habitus*', and he saw ascetic Protestantism as producing 'a *psychological vehicle* that *tended to create a typical conduct*'.[15] Weber's analysis was of the emergence of a particular type of *Lebensführung* or 'conduct of life', and his focus was on 'the aspect most difficult to grasp and "prove", relating to the inner habitus'.[16] The concept 'socialization' has emerged in its place, but it never properly dealt with the problem, because it left the door open for a continued re-emergence of arguments against the 'determinism' built into the concept of socialization.

This was why Elias frequently remarked on the continuing dichotomy of individual/society in sociological thought, to the frustration of many of his critics. Sociologists generally agree that individuals do not exist outside society, and that subjectivity is socially constructed. But the continued adherence to a theory of action, uninformed by psychology, smuggles the concept of an 'autonomous individual' opposing an 'autonomous society' back in via another route, re-embedding it within sociological thought at the very same time that a contrary theoretical position is taken up when the question is addressed overtly. Parsons read and utilized Freud later, but by then the damage had been done. Sociology had become organized around a dismissal of psychology, producing a schism in its understanding of human social life which Parsons' appropriation of psychoanalysis could only approach from the other side. The rejection of the concept of habit, remarks Camic, has 'left permanent effects on the inner conceptual structure of sociological thought'.[17] In other words, sociologists may *explicitly* agree that individuals are social beings, and thus become puzzled when Elias suggests they do not, but the *latent* structure of sociological theory continues to embody a continuing Hobbesian – and Parsonian – opposition between 'the individual' and 'society'. To put it as simply as possible, the huge and vital difference between Elias and Parsons was that Elias wrote Freud into his theory from the outset, whereas for Parsons psychoanalysis was a late addition to an already formulated sociological theory.

Second, Elias argued that the assumption that societies are normally well-integrated systems makes little sense, and that both social and system integration is emergent and contested. At first glance this looks like an echo of the standard criticisms of Parsons' approach from a conflict-theoretical position. But Elias's critique was aimed equally at Parsons' opponents, to the extent that they also neglected the *historical* interweaving of conflict and stability. For Elias it was important precisely to make the long-term processes of social integration and disintegration *themselves* the object of sociological study, rather than assuming a condition of either integration or conflict. It was the neglect of 'long-term processes of integration and disintegration as a theoretical and empirical topic of sociological enquiry'[18] which, Elias argued, had produced the opposition between conflict and consensus perspectives which dominated sociological debate in the 1960s and 1970s. Parsons had essentially rejected history, via his rejection of evolutionism; the famous opening line of *The Structure of Social Action* was a quotation from Harvard historian Crane Brinton, 'Who now reads

Spencer?'[19] Sociologists generally joined Parsons in his contempt for evolutionary theory, from a variety of perspectives; liberals would reject it because of its determinist implications, Marxists because of the neglect of class struggle and denial of the possibility of revolutionary transformations. Whatever the merits of a rejection of teleological evolutionary theory, in the process sociologists also forget about history altogether, and it is only in the last few decades that historical sociology has become taken more seriously. This relates back to the first point about human action, because it is only over time that one can trace the workings of habitus, and its re-formation over a number of generations. Elias's basic point is that habitus and culture are very slow to change, making it impossible to understand social life except over longer spans of time. A temporal dimension, in other words, is crucial to understanding the workings of human social life.

The theoretical position which Elias felt avoided these two mistakes – organizing sociology around a theory of 'action' and rejecting history – had the following basic elements:

1   an understanding of social life as the *unplanned and unintended outcome of the interweaving of intentional human actions*;
2   an approach to human beings as *interdependent*, forming *figurations* or networks with each other which connect the psychological with the social, or *habitus* with social relations;
3   a focus on *relations* rather than states;
4   a related concern with dynamic *processes* of development and change, rather than static structures;
5   an approach to sociology as the attempt to develop as '*adequate*' a relation to the real world as possible, namely one which 'works' best in the solution of basic problems of human existence and maximizes collective *control* over the human world.

UNPLANNED 'ORDER' AND THE QUESTION OF AGENCY

> From plans arising, yet unplanned
> By purpose moved, yet purposeless.[20]

Elias also sets out from the problem of how to explain the orderliness of social life, and sees sociology as fundamentally concerned with a 'problem of order'; but from a very different perspective to Parsons and, indeed, most sociologists today. In fact, the so-called 'Hobbesian problem of order', as Christopher Lloyd has pointed out, 'is in a sense not a problem for social science at all'.[21] It rests on the premise that it is possible for social order to 'disappear', for human relationships to be characterized by chaos, by the complete absence of orderliness. However, this is a false premise. While social formations can be relatively unstable, more or less integrated or disintegrated, there is always some form of social orderliness to human interaction. As Elias put it, 'The social life of people in societies always has, even in chaos or degeneration, in the greatest social disorder, a very particular form (*Gestalt*).'[22]

Elias did not see the very existence of 'social order' itself as problematic, saying that he understood the concept 'in the same sense that one talks of a natural order, in which decay and destruction as structured processes have their place alongside growth and synthesis, death and disintegration alongside birth and integration'.[23] He directed his attention to a very different question, namely, the apparent *independence* of social order from intentional human action. Where Parsons puzzled over how human beings formulated their ends and related them to their means, Elias went on to examine the relationship between the pursuit of those ends and the actual *outcome* of that pursuit in social life. For Elias, the question was: 'How does it happen at all that formations arise in the human world that no single human being has intended, and which yet are anything but cloud formations without stability or structure?'[24] It was the slowly dawning awareness from about the French Revolution onwards that, just as social life was not determined by God or supernatural forces, it was also not determined by the intentions of human beings, which Elias felt contributed to the emergence of sociology as a discipline. In his words:

> If one does not ask merely for a definition of society, but rather for the experiences which cradled a science of society, this was one of them: the experience that although people form societies and keep society moving by their actions and plans, at the same time society seems often to go its own way and, while being driven by those who form them, at the same time, seems to drive them.[25]

The thinkers who first contributed to this developing awareness included, suggested Elias, Adam Smith, Hegel, the Physiocrats, Malthus, Marx and Comte. Hegel's concept of the 'cunning of reason' was one of the first attempts to capture this 'ordered autonomy' of social life from the individuals who make it up:

> Again and again . . . people stand before the outcome of their own actions like the apprentice magician before the spirits he has conjured up and which, once at large, are no longer in his power. They look with astonishment at the convolutions and formations of the historical flow which they themselves constitute but do not control.[26]

Elias thus *recasts* the 'problem of order' as not being about the *possibility* of social order (Parsons), which needs no explanation, but about the relationship between social order and human intentionality, the actions of the human beings making it up. More precisely, the most acute problem for Elias was the apparent *lack* of relationship, the seemingly *alien* character of the social world to the individuals making it up.

Elias saw 'society' as consisting of the structured interweaving of the activity of interdependent human agents, all pursuing their own interests and goals, producing distinct social forms such as what we call 'Christianity', 'feudalism', 'patriarchy', 'capitalism', or whatever culture and nation we happen to be part of, which cannot be said to have been planned or intended by any individual or group. Weber's analysis of the roots of the spirit of rational capitalist accumulation in ascetic Protestantism provides a good example of the kind of 'blind' process Elias was talking about. Although human beings possess and conduct themselves with 'agency', then, this does not mean that they are the 'agents' or 'creators' of social life, which has a 'hidden order, not directly perceptible to the senses'.[27]

It is only in a limited sense, then, that people 'make their own history'. Elias formulated it as follows:

> It is simple enough: plans and actions, the emotional and rational impulses of individual people, constantly interweave in a friendly or hostile way. *This basic tissue resulting from many single plans and actions of men can give rise to changes and patterns that no individual person has planned or created. From this interdependence of people arises an order sui generis, an order more compelling and stronger than the will and reason of the individual people composing it.* It is this order of interweaving human impulses and strivings, this social order, which determines the course of historical change; it underlies the civilizing process.[28]

This conception has much in common with the notion of 'spontaneous order' usually attributed to Adam Ferguson and the Scottish Enlightenment theorists, although an earlier, theological version appeared in 1681, in the work of Bishop Jacques-Bénigne Bossuet.[29] There has been some discussion of the notion of the 'unintended consequences of human action', indeed Robert Merton published a short paper on the topic at the same time that *Über den Prozeß der Zivilisation* was being completed.[30] Friedrich von Hayek is also renowned for having explored the concept of 'spontaneous order' and also argued against the utility of planned intervention into economic and social processes.[31] However, Elias worked through the implications of the concept of 'unplanned order' far more systematically, and in relation to particular empirical examples. Instead of seeing unintentional outcomes merely as 'perverse' and mysterious effects of human action, he emphasized that 'unplanned development . . . is structured and correspondingly explainable'.[32] Rather than engaging in a polemical argument against communism and socialism, as von Hayek did, he analysed the *relationship* between intentional attempts to control and transform the social world and the long-term unplanned processes of development within which they take place.

Like Freud's demonstration that 'the ego is not master in its own house',[33] Elias's argument inflicts a narcissistic wound on modern sensibilities, because it emphasizes the extent to which the human world is resistant to direct control. 'It is frightening to realize that people form functional interconnections within which much of what they do is blind, purposeless and involuntary. It is much more reassuring to believe that history – which is of course always the history of particular human societies – has a meaning, a destination, perhaps even a purpose.'[34]

In analysing the relationship between intentional human action and unplanned surrounding social preconditions and outcomes, Elias emphasized, on the one hand, the dependence of any given individual, no matter how central a position they held, on the surrounding network of social, economic and political relations. 'No individual person, no matter how great his stature, how powerful his will, how penetrating his intelligence, can breach the autonomous laws of the human network from which his actions arise and into which they are directed.'[35] He indicated a very clear preference for understanding social transformations in terms of changes in social conditions, or in the structuring of social relationships, rather than attributing very much causal significance to the decisions and actions of particular, supposedly powerful individuals or groups.[36]

On the other hand, although within the broad sweep of history it is apparent how much individuals are buffeted by forces beyond their control, 'the person acting within the flow may have a better chance to see how much can depend on individual people in individual situations, despite the fixed general direction'.[37] It is equally unrealistic to believe 'that people are interchangeable, the individual being no more than the passive vehicle of a social machine'.[38] Elias saw social life as both 'firm' and 'elastic': 'Crossroads appear at which people must choose, and on their choices, depending on their social position, may depend either their immediate personal fate or that of a whole family, or, in certain situations, of entire nations or groups within them.'[39] Agency thus consisted of the strategic seizure of opportunities which arise for individuals and groups, but not in the actual creation of those opportunities, which 'are prescribed and limited by the specific structure of his society and the nature of the functions the people exercise within it'.[40] Moreover, once an opportunity is taken, human action 'becomes interwoven with those of others; it unleashes further chains of actions', the effects of which are based not on individual or group actors, but 'on the distribution of power and the structure of tensions within this whole mobile human network'.[41]

One of the primary focuses of sociological analysis is, then, the *relationships* between intentional, goal-directed human activities and the unplanned or unconscious process of interweaving with other such activities, past and present, and their consequences. Often Elias emphasized the unplanned character of social life, largely because he was concerned to counter the notion that there can ever be a direct and straightforward relationship between human action and its outcomes. However, all his observations taken together indicate a more complex understanding, for he always believed that improved human control of social life was the ultimate objective of sociological analysis. In his words, 'people can only hope to master and make sense out of these purposeless, meaningless functional interconnections if they can recognize them as relatively autonomous, distinctive functional inter-connections, and investigate them systematically'.[42] Elias saw an understanding of long-term unplanned changes as serving both 'an improved orientation' towards social processes which lie beyond human planning, and an improved understanding of those areas of social life which can be said to correspond to the goals and intentions of human action.[43] In relation to techno-logical change, he commented: 'From the viewpoint of a process theory what is interesting is the *interweaving of an unplanned process and human planning*.'[44]

INTERDEPENDENCE – FIGURATIONS – HABITUS

For Elias, the structure and dynamics of social life could only be understood if human beings were conceptualized as *interdependent* rather than autonomous, comprising what he called *figurations* rather than social systems or structures, and as characterized by socially and historically specific forms of *habitus*, or personality-structure. He emphasized seeing human beings in the plural rather than the singular, as part of collectivities, of groups and networks, and stressed that their very identity as unique individuals only existed within and through those networks or figurations.

The civilizing process itself, argued Elias, had produced a capsule or wall around individual experience dividing an inner world from the external world, individuals from society, and this had come to be reproduced within sociological theory itself. Rather than seeing individuals as ever having any autonomous, pre-social existence, Elias emphasized human beings' interde-pendence with each other, the fact that one can only become an individual human being within a web of social relationships and within a network of interdependencies with one's family, school, church, community, ethnic group, class, gender, work organization and so on. The essential 'relatedness' of human beings, said Elias, began with being born as a helpless infant, over which we have no control: 'Underlying all intended interactions of human beings is their unintended interdependence.'[45]

He developed this point in part through his critique of what he called the *homo clausus*, or 'closed personality' image of humans. Elias argued for a replacement of this *homo clausus* conception with its emphasis on autonomy, freedom and independent agency with:

> the image of man as an 'open personality' who possesses a greater or lesser degree of relative (but never absolute and total) autonomy vis-à-vis other people and who is, in fact, fundamentally oriented toward and dependent on other people throughout his life. The network of interdependencies among human beings is what binds them together. Such interdependencies are the nexus of what is here called the figuration, a structure of mutually oriented and dependent people. Since people are more or less dependent on each other first by nature and then through social learning, through education, socialization, and socially generated reciprocal needs, they exist, one might venture to say, only as pluralities, only in figurations.[46]

Elias introduced the concept of 'figuration' in the 1960s because it 'puts the problem of human interdependencies into the very heart of sociological theory'[47] and he hoped it would 'eliminate the antithesis . . . immanent today in the use of the words "individual" and "society"'.[48]

Before he started using the word 'configuration' in 1965 and then 'figuration' from 1969 onwards, the German concept he used was *Verflechtungsmechanismus*, or 'mechanism of interweaving'. Elias felt it expressed 'what we call "society" more clearly and unambiguously than the existing conceptual tools of sociology, as neither an abstraction of attributes of individuals existing without a society, nor a "system" or "totality" beyond individuals, but the network of interdependencies formed by individuals'.[49] Elias regarded societies as basically 'the processes and structures of interweaving, the figurations formed by the actions of inter-dependent people'.[50] He also believed that it made it easier to overcome the tendency to apparently deny human agency and individuality with the use of concepts like 'society' or 'social system'. Indeed, 'it sharpens and deepens our understanding of individuality if people are seen as forming figurations with other people'.[51]

Unlike 'system', it also did not convey the suggestion of harmony or integration characterizing the organic or machine analogy; it referred to 'harmonious, peaceful and friendly relationships between people, as well as to tense and hostile relationships'.[52] This means that figurations are always organized around the dynamic operation of *power*.

> At the core of changing figurations – indeed the very hub of the figuration process – is a fluctuating, tensile equilibrium, a balance of power moving to and fro, inclining first to one side and then to the other. This kind of fluctuating balance of power is a structural characteristic of the flow of every figuration.[53]

It was 'a generic concept for the pattern which interdependent human beings, as groups or as individuals, form with each other',[54] and Elias saw the analysis of the formation of dynamic figurations as 'one of the central questions, perhaps even *the* central question, of sociology'.[55] Indeed, 'it is this network of the functions which people have for each other, it and nothing else, that we call "society". It represents a special kind of sphere. Its structures are what we call "social structures". And if we talk of "social laws" or "social regularities", we are referring to nothing other than this: the autonomous laws of the relations between individual people.'[56]

He used the analogy of dance to illustrate the concept figuration, saying that 'the image of the mobile figurations of interdependent people on a dance floor perhaps makes it easier to imagine state, cities, families, and also capitalist, communist, and feudal systems as figurations'.[57] Although we might speak of 'dance in general', 'no one will imagine a dance as a structure outside the individual'. Dances can be danced by different people, 'but without a plurality of reciprocally oriented and dependent individuals, there is no dance'. Figurations, like dances, are thus 'relatively independent of the specific individuals forming it here and now, but not of individuals as such'.[58] In other words, although it is true that figurations 'have the peculiarity that, with few exceptions, they can continue to exist even when all the individuals who formed them at a certain time have died and been replaced by others',[59] they only exist in and through the activity of their participants. When that activity stops, the figuration stops, and the continued existence of the figuration is dependent on the continued participation of its constituent members, as the East European communist countries discovered in 1989. Figurations 'have a relative independence of particular individuals, but not of individuals as such'.[60]

It is difficult to overemphasize the significance of Elias's concept of figuration for sociological theory. Despite David Lockwood's argument that the distinction often made between *social integration* – 'the orderly or conflictual relationships between the *actors*' – and *system integration* – 'the orderly or conflictual relationships between the *parts*, of a social system' is 'wholly artificial',[61] sociologists, as we can see from the persistence of the agency/structure dichotomy, continue to operate as if the distinction was a real one. Nicos Mouzelis, for example, has argued recently for the retention of the concept 'structure' alongside that of 'figuration', suggesting that 'the complex ways in which figurations, institutional structures and structures in Giddens' sense are linked to each other constitutes one of the most interesting problems in sociological theory'.[62] This position rests on an understanding of 'figuration' as referring only to actor–actor relations, leaving the question of actor–institution or institution–institution relations unexamined, for which we need the concepts 'structure' and 'institutional structure'. However, it is unlikely that Elias would have accepted this interpretation of 'figuration'. His position was a more radical one, in that for him 'structures' *consisted* of actor–actor relations. In other words, 'figuration' was intended to capture exactly what is normally referred to with concepts such as 'structure' or 'system integration'. For Elias structures *are* figurations, they can only be understood as being *constituted* by acting human beings, and the concept figuration is intended to *dissolve* the distinction between system and social integration, not take its place within it.

The dynamics of figurations are also dependent on the formation of a shared social *habitus* or personality make-up which constitutes the collective basis of individual human conduct. In his words:

> This make-up, the social habitus of individuals forms, as it were, the soil from which grow the personal characteristics through which an individual differs from other members of his society. In this way something grows out of the common language which the individual shares with others and which is certainly a component of his social habitus – a more or less individual style, what might be called an unmistakable individual handwriting that grows out of the social script.[63]

Elias gave the example of the concept of 'national character', which he called 'a habitus problem *par excellence*'.[64] He also referred to is as 'second nature', or 'an automatic, blindly functioning apparatus of self-control'.[65] The organization of psychological make-up into a *habitus* was also, for Elias, a continuous *process* which began at birth and continued throughout a person's childhood and youth. It is, he wrote,

> the web of social relations in which the individual lives during his more impressionable phase, during childhood and youth,

> which imprints itself upon his unfolding personality where it has its counterpart in the relationship between his controlling agencies, super-ego and ego, and his libidinal impulses. The resulting balance between controlling agencies and drives on a variety of levels determines how an individual person steers himself in his relations with others; it determines that which we call, according to taste, habits, complexes or personality structure.[66]

Moreover, the development of habitus continued through a person's life, 'for although the self-steering of a person, malleable during childhood, solidifies and hardens as he grows up, it never ceases entirely to be affected by his changing relations with others throughout his life'.[67]

Finally, the ways in which the formation of habitus changed over time, what Elias called *psychogenesis*, could also only be properly understood in connection with changes in the surrounding social relations, or *sociogenesis*. He argued against the disciplinary separation of psychology, sociology and history as follows:

> The structures of the human psyche, the structures of human society and the structures of human history are indissolubly complementary, and can only be studied in conjunction with each other. They do not exist and move in reality with the degree of isolation assumed by current research. They form, with other structures, the subject matter of the single human science.[68]

In his critique of Lloyd de Mause's psychogenetic theory of the history of childhood, Elias said that 'psychogenetic studies alone, without the closest connection with sociogenetic studies, are hardly suitable for revealing the structures of social processes. This is only possible with a theory of civilization which links psychogenetic and sociogenetic aspects to each other.'[69] The formation of habitus is a function of social interdependencies, which vary as the structure of a society varies. 'To the variations in this structure,' wrote Elias, 'correspond the differences in personality structure than can be observed in history.'[70] While he used the notion of 'correspondence' between habitus and social structure in *The Civilizing Process*,[71] later he modified his position to accommodate the possibility that social habitus might change more slowly than the surrounding social relations.[72] Our 'whole outlook on life' said Elias, 'continues to be psychologically tied to yesterday's social reality, although today's and tomorrow's reality already differs greatly from yesterday's'.[73]

SOCIAL LIFE AS RELATIONS

Elias consistently maintained that it was necessary for sociologists to avoid seeing social life in terms of states, objects or things, what Georgy Lukács called the *reificiation* of what are in fact dynamic social relationships. His attempt to transcend reification in sociological theory consisted of a double movement: the first was towards a consistent emphasis on social life as *relational*, and the second was an insistence on its *processual* character. We will look at the first in this section and the second in the following section. It is important to emphasize both sides of this double movement away from reification, because many sociologists undertake one or the other,[74] but very few pursue both. All of the rest of his theory flowed in one way or another from this starting point.

The principle is simple enough, that it is necessary in sociology 'to give up thinking in terms of single, isolated substances and to start thinking in terms of relationships and functions'.[75] A 'person' or 'individual' is thus not a self-contained entity or unit, she or he does not exist 'in themselves', they only exist as elements of sets of relations with other individuals. The same applies to families, communities, organizations, nations, economic systems, in fact to any aspect of the world, human or natural, for the concept arose from Einstein's physics. Relations between people, the ties binding them to each other are, for Elias, the primary object of sociological study, the very stuff of historical change:

> What changes is the way in which people are bonded to each other. This is why their behaviour changes, and why their consciousness and their drive-economy, and, in fact, their personality structure as a whole, change. The 'circumstances' which change are not something which comes upon men from 'outside': they are the relationships between people themselves.[76]

The explanation of any sociological question thus has to focus on the social relations composing the object of study, rather than any of its elements in isolation. This applies even to understanding individual experience; as Elias put it: 'Even the nature and form of his solitude, even what he feels to be his "inner life", is stamped by the history of his relationships – by the structure of the human network in which, as one of its nodal points, he develops and lives as an individual.'[77] We have to start, Elias said, 'from the structure of the relations *between* individuals in order to understand the "psyche" of the individual person'.[78]

Recently the significance of this has been underlined by Pierre Bourdieu, who defines this form of perception as thinking in terms of *fields*, a mode of thought which 'requires a conversion of one's entire usual vision of the social world, a vision which is interested only in those things which are visible'.[79] Referring to Elias, he points out that thinking non-relationally also has the effect of treating social units as if they were themselves human actors, and mentions the possible 'endless list of mistakes, mystifications or mystiques created by the fact that the words designating institutions or groups, State, bourgeoisie, Employers, Church, Family and School, can be constituted . . . as historical subjects capable of posing and realizing their own aims'.[80]

What Elias found most important about relationships between people was the way in which they were constituted as *power* relations, so that he develops this argument in most detail with reference to 'the relational character of power'.[81] He felt that there was a particularly strong tendency to reify power, to treat it as an object which was possessed to a greater or lesser extent. 'The whole sociological and political discussion on power', he wrote, 'is marred by the fact that the dialogue is not consistently focused on power balances and power ratios, that is, on aspects of relationships, but rather on power as if it were a thing.'[82] If we see it more as a relation, it also becomes possible to recognize that questions of power are quite distinct from questions of 'freedom' and 'domination', and that all human relationships are relations of power.

Building on both Hegel's famous discussion of the master–slave relation and Georg Simmel's reflections on power and domination, Elias wrote:

> The master has power over his slave, but the slave also has power over his master, in proportion to his function for the master – his master's dependence on him. . . . In this respect, simply to use the word 'power' is likely to mislead. We say that a person possesses great power, as if power were a thing he carried about in his pocket. This use of the word is a relic of magico-mythical ideas. Power is not an amulet possessed by one person and not by another; it is a structural characteristic of human relationships – of *all* human relationships.[83]

He went on to refer consistently to power in terms of *power-ratios* or 'shifting balances of tensions',[84] and regarded these concepts as the best successors to debates about freedom and determinism. Referring to Sartre's conception of existential freedom, he said that the recognition that all human beings possess some degree of freedom or autonomy 'is sometimes romantically idealized as proving the metaphysical freedom of man', its popularity arising primarily from its emotional appeal.[85] However, he argued that it was important to go beyond thinking in terms of a fictional antithesis between 'freedom' and 'determinism' – fictional because of human beings' essential interdependence – and move to thinking in terms of power-balances.

He stressed the *reciprocal* workings of power, so that within the network of relations binding the more and less powerful to each other, apparently less powerful groups also exercise a 'boomerang effect' back on those with greater power-chances. As he put it, 'in one form or another the constraints that more powerful groups exert on less powerful ones recoil on the former as constraints of the less powerful on the more powerful and also as compulsions to self-constraint'.[86] This was, he felt, a problem with concepts like 'rule' or 'authority', since they 'usually make visible only the pressures exerted from above to below, but not those from below to above'.[87] He gave the example of the relation between parents and children: parents clearly have greater power-chances than their children, but because children fulfil particular functions and needs for their parents, they also have power over their parents, such as calling them to their aid by crying, or requiring them to reorganize their lives.[88]

To say that the less powerful also exercise power over the more powerful within a power relation, however, only applies to the *internal* dynamics of that relationship, but not to any capacity to transform it. For example, when one of his assistants, Angela Rijnen, suggested to him that slaves in ancient Rome could have acted on their masters' dependence on them, refused to co-operate on a collective basis, and thus escaped their enslavement, Elias became furious: 'How dare you say something like that? . . . You must know that the figuration was not of a type that slaves could resist it?'[89] Unlike Foucault, then, Elias did not conceptualize power relations in terms of an opposition between power and resistance, but as consisting of more or less even 'balances' or 'ratios'.

Although Elias's work has much in common with that of Herbert Blumer and symbolic interactionist writers, the comparison should be approached with caution, since Elias was never satisfied with the concept of 'social interaction'. He argued that, at best, it only 'scratches the surface of the relatedness of human beings',[90] to the extent that it fails to move beyond the *homo clausus* model of human beings as possessing some basic identity prior to their interactions with others. Social interaction creates 'the impression of something arising solely from the initiative of two originally independent individuals – an *ego* and an *alter*, an "I" and an "other" – or from the meeting of a number of originally independent individuals'.[91] He felt that without an adequate understanding of the essential *interdependence* of human beings within a wide network of relationships, even theories of interaction would posit a pre-social individual who only became social when they engaged in social interaction.[92] The parallel between Elias's approach and symbolic interactionism only holds, then, to the extent that this objection is met.

AGAINST PROCESS-REDUCTION

The second step Elias took away from the reification of social life was to see it as having an inherently *processual* character, and this needs to be seen in combination with his emphasis on relationism. Figurations of interdependent individuals and groups can only be properly understood as existing over time, in a constant process of dynamic flux and greater or lesser transformation. The analysis of the interrelationships between intentional action and unplanned social processes had to be undertaken over periods of time, for as Johan Goudsblom has put it, 'yesterday's unintended social consequences are today's unintended social conditions of 'intentional human actions'.[93] Elias spoke of the 'the transformational impetus (*Wandlungsimpetus*) of every human society', and regarded 'the immanent impetus towards change as an integral moment of every social structure and their temporary stability as the expression of an impediment to social change'.[94]

A historical approach to sociological analysis was, in fact, self-evident to most sociologists up to World War II. In *The Civilizing Process* itself the main disciplinary argument was with psychology, which was why like-minded writers such as Mannheim always spoke of the need for a 'historical psychology';[95] there was no need to argue for a 'historical sociology'. However, Elias pointed out that in the course of the twentieth century a momentum had been building up against theories of 'progress' and 'evolution', especially their normative and teleological dimensions, their assumption that all social change was essentially 'progressive' and that the current form of society was the apex of human development. In the process, social scientists lost interest in development of any sort. Rather than merely rejecting the normative and teleological *elements* of evolutionary theories, the whole idea of examining long-term processes of change became unfashionable, and most sociologists stopped concerning themselves with a historical approach to their discipline altogether. In Elias's words:

> it is not simply the ideological elements in the nineteenth century sociological concept that have been called into question, but the concept of development itself, the very consideration of problems of long-term social development, of sociogenesis and psychogenesis. In a word, the baby has been thrown out with the bathwater.[96]

The notion that 'present social conditions represent an instant of a continuous process which, coming from the past, moves on through present times towards a future as yet unknown, appears to have vanished'.[97] In 1970 Elias pointed out that where the concept 'development' was used, it was restricted to non-Western, 'underdeveloped' or 'developing' countries, implying that Western, highly industrialized nations were not in a developing state.[98]

The expression Elias used to identify the tendency in sociological thought which he was arguing against was *Zustandsreduktion* – literally, 'reduction to states', although in English he preferred 'process-reduction', i.e., the 'reduction of processes to static condi-tions'.[99] A manifestation of process-reduction was sociologists' turning away from historical analysis, the emphasis by both functionalists and structuralists on synchronic rather than dia-chronic analysis, and the assumption that stability was the normal condition of social life, and change a 'disruption' of a normal state of equilibrium. By 'long-term' Elias meant periods of not less than three generations.[100]

Just as individuals, families, communities, and so on, should be conceived as embedded within a network of relations, rather than being seen as isolated objects, Elias argued that they should also be seen as *dynamic*, in a state of flux and change, as processes. Individuals, for example, rather than having a fixed identity,

> are born as infants, have to be fed and protected for many years by their parents or other adults, who slowly grow up, who then provide for themselves in this or that social position, who may marry and have children of their own, and who finally die. So an individual may justifiably be seen as a self-transforming person who, as it is sometimes put, goes through a process.[101]

Indeed, suggested Elias, although it is not how we are used to thinking about ourselves, 'it would be more appropriate to say that a person is constantly in movement; he not only goes through a process, he *is* a process'.[102] We can only understand and explain any given sociological problem if it is seen as the outcome of some long-term process of development, if we trace its *sociogenesis*.

Instead of speaking of static 'states' or phenomena such as capitalism, rationality, bureaucracy, modernity, postmodernity, Elias would always wish to identify their processual character, so that he would think in terms of rationalization, modernization, bureaucratization, and so on. Often it is difficult to come up with the appropriate concept. For example, 'capitalism' is difficult to render in this way – but the point is to attempt a conceptualization along these lines, to identify the process underlying what one was studying. If, for example, one observes what appear to be a large number of single parents in Western societies, a productive approach for Elias would be to look for the long-term trends in marriage and fertility, to see how this current phenomenon fits in with other processes of social development, in order to possibly explain its occurrence. This example also illustrates Elias's emphasis on the existence of a *plurality* of processes, all of which interweave with each other, with no causal primacy being given to any one of them. Transformations in social relationships are thus intertwined with a variety of other processes of change: economic, political, psychological, geographical, and so on. The main long-term trends Elias concentrated on included increasing social differentiation, industrialization, urbanization, political centralization, integration from smaller to larger social units, state formation and nation building, functional democratization, psychologization and rationalization – these will be discussed in the next chapter.

Social processes had no particular beginning; he said: 'Wherever we start, there is movement, something that went before.'[103] They also have no end, Elias always assumed that we find ourselves in the *middle* of any given process, and that the point of looking to where it came from was to provide some sense of its future development. He said a number of things about the question of *directionality*: often he seemed to insist that the *overall* direction of a long-term trend was all that mattered, and that any divergences from this direction would only be temporary interruptions to the broader tendency. For example in a letter to Gerhard Schmied in 1982, he said of the Roman Empire that it 'was in turn again only the apex of an integrative movement' and that 'All in all, there is only one single developmental process. One should demonstrate it in all states in the world.'[104] It is this type of argument which leads some critics to regard Elias as a unilinear evolutionist. However, he also said that 'two main directions in the structural changes of societies may be distinguished: those tending toward increased differentiation and integration, and those tending toward decreasing differentiation and integration',[105] leading commentators such as Peter Burke to describe his theory as *multilinear*.[106] Any given trend 'is always linked to counter-trends. A trend might remain dominant for a long time; then a counter-trend can again completely or partially gain the upper hand.'[107] This perspective was developed in more detail in his work on twentieth-century German history, and the notion of *de*civilizing processes which underlay particular historical events like the Holocaust. These arguments will also be examined in the next chapter.

A major difference between Elias's approach to long-term social processes and earlier theories of evolutionary change was that he did not think it possible to identify the course of development which *had* to take place. His explanatory concern was primarily *retrospective*, focusing on how:

> *a figuration had to arise out of a certain earlier figuration or even out of a particular type of sequential series of figurations, but [it] does not assert that the earlier figurations had necessarily to change into the later ones.*[108]

One could not say that figuration C necessarily had to emerge from figurations A and B, only that C was *made possible* by the emergence of A and B, that A and B were the *necessary preconditions* for C. Figuration C was thus only one of the possible successors to A and B, and there is never a necessity or teleology to the social development.

Although Elias did distance himself from theories of social progress which simply assumed that all social change was progressive, he did feel that, overall, humanity was in fact progressing. It is important to bear his fundamentally *ambiguous* attitude to progress in mind, because it helps explain why so many of his critics accuse him of reverting to the ninteenth-century evolutionary perspectives. For example, in 1977 he wrote:

the twentieth century is an epoch of the greatest experiments and innovations. . . . Much of what people in earlier times only dreamed of has become 'do-able'. Human knowledge – not only about interconnections in the non-human, natural world, but also about people themselves, on the individual as well as social level – is far more extensive than in the past. The conscious, planned concern with improvement of the social order and human living conditions – as inadequate as it is – has never been greater than it is today.[109]

He was also confident that human beings have gradually developed more control over the natural world, and that this increased control could easily be put in the category of 'progress'. When challenged about his attitude to the control of the natural world by a Dutch interviewer, he said: 'We can't go back to nature, that's a dreadful idea, nature is wild, blind, angry, sometimes beautiful. . . . The most important thing we have is what we make out of nature, not nature itself.'[110] Despite the barbarism which Western 'civilized' people were capable of, for Elias this meant merely that 'we have not learnt to control ourselves and nature enough', for he was insistent that the contemporary world was considerably less brutal and violent than it had been in the ancient or medieval periods. He felt that relations between classes, men and women, superordinates and subordinates, adults and children, were gradually becoming increasingly equal and democratic, and that the point of identifying those instances where this was not the case was to *further* the process of 'functional democratization', not to suggest its impossibility.

On the other hand, he did also argue that processes of integration could at any time be accompanied by those of disintegration, civilizing processes by decivilizing processes,[111] and he placed more emphasis on these in his later work, such as *The Germans*. Elias should be read both ways, as optimistic about the progress of humanity, and as acutely aware of how easily we can descend to barbaric cruelty. The death of his mother in Auschwitz was a permanent reminder of that, so he can not be accused of being unaware of the dark side of Western civilization. The question of how his attitude to progress can be evaluated will be addressed in the next chapter.

SOCIOLOGY AND 'OBJECT-ADEQUACY'

Standing in the middle of social relations and processes of long-term development are, of course, human beings, thinking about the world around them, orienting themselves towards it, and acting on it, developing knowledge about their world. For Elias, sociology itself also had to be considered part of an ongoing social process of the development of knowledge.[112] Elias regarded sociology as a particular example of people's on-going attempts to gain better control over their own lives. Just as the natural sciences provided improved orientation towards and control over the natural world, sociology's task was to achieve the same in relation to the social world. Its method, however, was quite different from the natural sciences, because sociologists were themselves part of what they studied, namely, human society. They were what Elias called 'involved' in society.[113] The aim of social scientific analysis, however, was to gain workable knowledge about the social world with which to observe it from the outside with a measure of 'detachment'. Elias thus argued that sociological analysis moves constantly between these two poles of 'involvement' and 'detachment', between an expression of the sociologist's *subjective* experience of the world, and the attempt to transcend that experience in gaining an *objective, scientific* perspective. Involvement and detachment were not mutually exclusive for Elias. The point was more that people constantly moved between the two poles.

Non-scientific, magical-mythical knowledge is essentially knowledge based on beliefs, wishes and articles of faith rather than observation of the real world and its interaction with human beings. Scientific knowledge, on the other hand, is constantly tied to its objects and tested against the criterion of what Elias called 'object-adequacy' or 'reality-congruence'. It was precisely because social life developed to a large extent 'blindly', independently of human intentions, that:

> The task of sociological research is *to make these blind, uncontrolled processes more accessible to human understanding* by explaining them, and to enable people to orientate themselves within the interwoven social web – which, though created by their own needs and actions, is still opaque to them – and so better to control it.[114]

Elias felt that much of the sociology of knowledge was in danger of falling into a relativistic position, where all human ideas were seen as socially produced, as ideology, and there were no criteria for identifying 'advances' in knowledge. His position is basically that of 'neo-realism', which Christopher Lloyd has summarised as follows:

> a line of reasoning stemming partly from Quine, and including (in different ways) Putnam, Harré and Madden, Shapere, Boyd, and Hesse, has cogently shown that, although our investigations of both the world and our ways of knowing about it do always have to be made within particular ways of knowing, there has clearly been some progress in discovering the causal structure of the world. People collectively over time have been able to improve their understandings of nature and society and to exert some control over them accordingly.[115]

This conception of *relative* improvement in the correspondence between human knowledge and the world of experience was important to Elias, for he opposed what he called 'rough dichotomies like "true" and "false"'.[116] The aim of scientific research was 'to develop a steadily expanding body of theories or models and an equally expanding body of observations about specific events by means of a continuous, critical confrontation to greater and greater congruity with each other'.[117] Elias was critical of Mannheim's approach to knowledge on the grounds that 'he did not go beyond a critical unmasking of other people's thought structures as ideologies'.[118] He felt that knowledge could be 'reality-revealing as well as reality-concealing' and, drawing an analogy with a doctor's understanding of the human body, argued that non-ideological knowledge was possible: 'Why should one not be in a position to produce non-ideological knowledge of human society?'[119]

There was rarely place made for values, ethical principles or political beliefs in Elias's conception of science. He often complained of the transformation of an ethical 'ought' into a supposedly scientific 'is', and said that sociologists should refrain from expressing their own value judgements.

> Sociologists ought rather to free themselves from the notion that there is or even will be any necessary correspondence between the society they are investigating and their own social beliefs, their wishes and hopes, their moral predilections or their conceptions of what is just and humane.[120]

When confronted with the observation, as he often was by his colleagues in Leicester, that scientific knowledge is inevitably structured and permeated by scientists' values and world views, 'that we are all engaged and involved', he interpreted this as an argument for 'a kind of pre-established harmony between social ideal and social reality'.[121]

CRITIQUES

A number of writers have put forward a variety of criticisms of Elias's general approach to sociology, and they can be grouped roughly into four categories:

1   the question of the *distinctiveness* of Elias's perspective;
2   his treatment of human *agency*;
3   his emphasis on historical *continuity* at the expense of discontinuity; and
4   his understanding of the *politics of knowledge.*

All of them usefully illuminate Elias's relationship to wider sociological thought. There are other criticisms which focus more specifically on his theory of the civilizing process, but they are dealt with in the next chapter.

The first type of criticism can be grouped under the heading of Lewis Coser's comment that 'Elias tends to ram in open doors'.[122] They revolve around similar observations about the validity of Elias's critique of what he presented as the prevailing paradigms in sociological thought, and the actual distinctiveness of his approach in comparison to other sociological approaches. Zygmunt Bauman, for example, suggests that 'Elias's objection to radical individualism would easily command broad support'[123] in sociology, and Derek Layder points out that the argument against the dichotomy between individual and society can be found in early sociologists such as Cooley, who said: 'A separate individual is an abstraction unknown to experience, and so likewise is society when regarded as something apart from individuals.'[124] American sociologists like Louis Wirth who had read Simmel also came to a similar 'relational' perspective on social life.[125] Indeed, one could argue that Elias's attempt to demonstrate that Durkheim had 'struggled in vain'[126] with the problem of how to conceptualize individuals and society was never very convincing. Alongside the parallels between Durkheim's and Freud's view of social life,[127] there are also strong similarities between Durkheim's work and Elias's, especially when one reads Durkheim the way American sociologists like Harry Alpert did in the 1930s and 1940s.[128]

A variety of sociological writers such as ethnomethodologists, phenomenologists and symbolic interactionists[129] also emphasize the dynamic, emergent character of social life, and argue against seeing social reality as independent from human practices.[130] They had also read Simmel, and in Goffman's case, Elias. Similar relational approaches can be found in a wide variety of other writers and schools of thought, including R.D. Laing, *Gestalt* psychology, field theory, Jean Piaget and Rom Harré. Elias's critique of the concept 'interaction' is basically the same as that of the 'transactionalism' of John Dewey and Arthur Bentley. They distinguished between 'interaction' – where independent elements are seen as engaging in a relation with each other, so that the elements are primary and the relation secondary – and 'transaction' – where the elements in a social process *emerge from* the relations between them, so that the relation is primary, and the elements secondary.[131] Indeed, Arthur Bentley, who had been taught by Dilthey and Simmel, suggested that human activities should be regarded as 'interlaced':

> That, however, is a bad manner of expression. For *the interlacing itself is the activity*. We have one great moving process to study, and of this great moving process it is impossible to state any part except as valued in terms of the other parts.[132]

Bentley thus came to much the same position as Elias, stressing both the 'interlacing' (interweaving) of human activity and its dynamic, processual character. One could also draw parallels with the ideas of network theorists, who focus on the 'pattern of ties' and networks of relations linking the members of a social system.[133] For network analysis, 'the organization of social relations [is] a central concept in analysing the structural properties of the networks within which individual actors are embedded, and for detecting emergent social phenomena that have no existence at the level of the individual actor',[134] an approach which bears a strong resemblance to Elias's use of the concept of figurations.

It may, then, be fair to say that *nothing* in Elias's approach cannot be found in some other school of sociological or psychological thought. Certainly we should reject Elias's self-portrayal as the sole, lonely representative of particular ideas, and his refusal explicitly to acknowledge any alliance with other sociological theorists. His preference for radically *transcending* current sociological debates over *participating* in them tends to discourage theoretical debate, and there is a distinct aggressiveness in his attitude to other theoretical positions – Kilminster referred to it as assuming he had theoretical 'right of way'[135] – which understandably produces a hostile response among those trained in different theoretical traditions. For Dick Pels, the treatment of other schools of thought by both Elias and many of his followers is 'expressive of the soft-spoken violence of an unacknowledged politics of theory'.[136]

However, two arguments emerge once we reach this point. First, Elias's contribution may lie more in the way he went about his *synthesis* or perhaps *integration* of what tend to operate as distinct sociological perspectives. For example, symbolic interactionists have a similar view of human conduct and social relationships, but they rarely develop a *historical* dimension to their analyses. The concept of 'spontaneous order' may appear in the work of writers such as von Hayek and Popper, and there may be occasional mention of the 'unintended consequences of human action', but generally the implications of the 'distance' between human action and its outcomes in social life remain poorly understood and researched. The significance for sociology of the Scottish Enlightenment theorists – which Elias's work can be seen as an extension of – also remains underappreciated.[137] Elias's work actually looks more impressive once we *reject* his view of himself as a lonely maverick, and see the parallels with other sociological thinkers as precisely its *strength*, making it a complex synthesis of disparate sociological traditions. It will probably be most useful simply to ignore the presentation of Elias's sociology as emerging like Athene from Zeus' head, and instead follow his actual practice up to *The Civilizing Process*: using a careful and thorough reading of the main streams of sociological thought as a foundation for a theory of human society which synthesizes their various contributions.[138]

Second, although most of the arguments deployed by Elias can be found in other sociologists' work, in his critiques Elias was concerned primarily with the 'dominant' or 'prevailing' mode of sociological thought, and the question is then whether sociologists have consistently practised the principles which various predecessors have articulated. In particular, there is the possibility that specific forms of perception, apparently vanquished in explicit arguments and in the relevant sections of the textbooks, simply reappear in another form, built into the structure of sociological thought with different labels attached. One key example here is the question of whether sociologists continue to see 'the individual' and 'society' as separate entities. Many critics suggest that this battle was won long ago, and the transcendence of the dichotomy is simply part of sociology's inheritance. If we can read it in Marx, Weber, Durkheim and Simmel, why repeat the argument? The problem, as Charles Camic has shown,[139] is that the early sociologists can be read in a variety of ways, and the effect of both Parsons' construction of 'the sociological tradition' and the criticisms of it has been, until only quite recently, to perceive human conduct in a way which reproduces the individual/society dichotomy. Randall Collins has demonstrated that the conception of sociological thought as divided between a concern for either 'structure' or 'agency' similarly reproduced an ancient opposition between 'freedom' and 'determinism'. Donald Levine has also pointed out that Parsons' concern to compete with Howard Becker for the 'importation' of German sociology into the USA contributed to the long neglect of Simmel in American sociology, and helped suppress the kind of relational view espoused by writers such as Louis Wirth from sociological consciousness.[140] Concepts and modes of perception have a habit of either rising, phoenix-like, from the ashes, or remaining detached from the real practice of thinking. Elias's arguments about problems in sociological thought need to be addressed at the level of its deep, underlying structure rather than merely its surface arguments, and from that perspective they retain much of their force. If they did not, we would not still be puzzling over the supposed distinctions between agency and structure, social and system integration, or micro and macro approaches to sociology.[141]

A second type of criticism concerns Elias's approach to human agency within figurations and long-term, 'blind' social processes. Bauman commented that 'Elias encourages his followers to close their eyes to the active, creative role of the individual or collective *subject* of knowledge,'[142] and Dennis Smith suggested that 'his approach leaves unresolved an important contradiction concerning the human capacity for choice and evaluation'.[143] What distinguished Elias from writers such as Marcuse, Habermas and Moore, said Smith, was 'his "bleaching out" of the evaluating, choosing side of humanity'.[144] Hans Haferkamp also felt uneasy about the emphasis which Elias placed on the unplanned and 'blind' character of social development: 'Elias does not give much weight to the success of intentions and plans in this framework. Nor does he check to see when the planning of associations of actions has been successful . . . there have been many situations where micro- or macro-social actors have succeeded in their intentions and plans.'[145]

On the one hand, to the extent that 'agency' is conceived as somehow 'oppositional' to, or 'autonomous' from, social determination, this kind of criticism merely reinforces Elias's assertion that the individual/society dichotomy is still a problem in sociological thought. On the other hand, the more sophisticated versions of this argument do touch on some limitations in Elias's work concerning his concentration on the 'blind' character of social development. However, the response from the mature Elias would be that where one lays the emphasis would depend on what was being explained. He did speak of the 'interweaving' of successfully executed intentional action with long-term processes which by definition could not be regarded as 'planned', because they stretched over at least three generations, beyond the life-span of any individual human being. For Elias, Haferkamp's argument would be less significant in relation to the questions he was addressing himself to: processes of state formation, social and economic differentiation, democratization and rationalization, and so on. However, the significant point to which Haferkamp's argument draws our attention, and which would constitute an important modification of Elias's approach, is the notion of *collective agency* – what Haferkamp called the intentions of *macro-social actors*. If intention and agency can be ascribed to macro-social 'actors' such as an organization or some other collective entity – say, a nation–state, a Church or an economic organization, a nation – then its life span would stretch over the kinds of periods Elias regarded as long term, and it would be more possible to speak of the realization of intentions and plans in human history. This certainly seems to be the direction Elias was moving towards in his later work in *The Germans*.

Otherwise, however, Elias would have been quite unapologetic about his approach to human agency. He would have regarded claims like: 'The residuum of human autonomy and creativity must be reclaimed for social theory otherwise the full implications of human agency will be totally eclipsed'[146] as reflecting a continuing romanticism about individual 'freedom', and as a misinterpretation of the reality of human social existence. Elias never challenged the idea that human beings act creatively, with conscious intent, and that their actions cannot be simply read off in a deterministic fashion from their surrounding social context. This is different, however, from attributed *effectivity* to their action. It is the effects of human action which have to be regarded as determined by the way a combination of actions interweave with each other, frequently in *conflict* and *competition* with each other. The process by which the actions of various human agents, individual and collective, combine and interpenetrate with each other, by definition lies beyond the control of any of the participating 'actors'. Rather than 'bleaching out' human choice and evaluation, Elias's position concerning agency is simply one about the 'logic of collective action', about the real effects those choices and evaluations actually have once they enter social life, especially while human groups continue to compete with each other. It is the dynamics of *competition, conflict* and *interweaving* which constitutes the 'blindness' of social development and restricts the effectivity of human agency.

Third, Pierre Bourdieu believes that Elias's emphasis on long-term social processes focuses more than he would like to on continuous historical developments, at the expense of attending to the particular discontinuities and breaks in long-term trends. Bourdieu remarks that 'Elias is also more sensitive than I am to continuity. Historical analysis of long-term trends is always liable to hide critical breaks.' Referring to Elias's 'Essay on sport and violence',[147] Bourdieu says that it 'carries the danger of masking the fundamental ruptures introduced, among other things, by the rise of educational systems, English colleges and boarding schools, etc., and by the subsequent constitution of a relatively autonomous "space of sports"'.[148] Generally it is true that Elias's position has been to regard such ruptures as less important than the long-term trends, but he did speak of 'spurts' and 'shifts' in various social processes, and Bourdieu's examples in relation to sport constitute exactly that kind of 'accelerated' development rather than any real discontinuity. Indeed, Elias himself developed an increasing sensitivity to more serious ruptures and breaks as he spoke more of 'counter-trends' and 'the bi-polar character of social processes'.[149] Derek Layder also suggests that in his critique of process-reduction Elias overlooks the fact that processes actually consist of, and can only be analysed by social scientists as *sequences* of static states, but Elias was well aware of this, and would speak of his analysis in terms of 'stills' in a movie.[150] Elias's point was to be more aware than most sociologists seemed to be, that the 'movie' they were looking at was a long one.

Finally, there are reasons to be cautious about Elias's approach to the politics of social scientific knowledge as well as the practicalities of sociological research. Elias maintained that sociologists should see themselves as 'destroyers of myths'. By developing an alternative ('scientific') vocabulary and conceptual apparatus which is more responsive to the social world we are trying to analyse, it will be possible to make apparently mysterious, 'blind' processes of social development more accessible to human understanding and control. In this sense, he takes up the same position as the majority of sociologists, who argue that sociological knowledge is distinct from everyday understandings of personal experience, and provides an insight into the unconscious, invisible dynamics of social life. However, it is here that Elias's 'detachment' produces a range of problems, since the production of de-mythologizing knowledge is itself a political exercise – myths are not merely 'mistakes' or even the accompaniments of earlier forms of social life, they are located within very specific relations of power and play a role within those power relations concerning 'the *legitimate* representation of the social world'.[151] For example, in response to Elias's interest in maximizing control over the social world, the obvious question to ask is: 'Who's control over whom?' This is why Bourdieu argues:

> The idea of a neutral science is a fiction, and an interested fiction, which enables one to pass as scientific a neutralized and euphemized form of the dominant representation of the social world. . . . By uncovering the social mechanisms which ensure the maintenance of the established order and whose properly symbolic efficacy rests on the misconception of their logic and effects, *social science necessarily takes sides in political struggles.*[152]

Elias does argue for a *reflexive* approach to sociological research and theorizing, for linking the development of knowledge to surrounding developments in social relations, and for making sociological method itself part of the object of sociological research. However, his essentially Weberian position on scientific 'value-freedom' and his emphasis on 'detachment' regarding the politics and social context of sociological theory and research give us very little purchase on either the rough and tumble of social scientific practice, or the impact and effects on social life of sociology itself.

Derek Layder also points out that Elias never properly clarifies the question of the *validity* of scientific knowledge, particularly the question of how the 'object-adequacy' of knowledge is to be determined, according to which criteria and by whom. Using a concept like 'object-adequate' instead of 'true', and posing a continuum between 'less' and 'more' object-adequate rather than a dichotomy between truth and falsity, does not solve the problem of how we are to decide what is more or less 'adequate'. Using criteria like the 'survival value' of knowledge, or its contribution to 'control' of the natural and social world, also raises as many questions as it answers: what constitutes 'survival'? 'Control'? As Dick Pels remarks, Elias 'remains happily innocent of the modern social studies of science both before and after the Strong programme'. Apart from the early Popper, 'there has been no serious engagement with any of the major positions in contemporary philosophy or sociology of knowledge'.[153] This does not mean that it is clear, as Layder suggests, that Elias's epistemology can simply be dismissed as 'sophisticated empiricism', or that his 'naive objectivistic confidence about the immediate accessibility of reality and the avoidability of interest, speaks in an anachronistic voice from the past worthy to be buried',[154] since there are similarities with quite strong positions within the sociology of science debates, such as neo-realism. He argued himself that knowledge was located within relations of power and took up an institutionalized position within social relationships, albeit without extending those arguments to his own concept of 'object-adequacy'. However, we can agree that Elias's sociology of knowledge is one of the more problematic aspects of his work, one which could only benefit from a dialogue with the extensive work done on the sociology of science.

So far I have sketched the basic elements of Elias's theory of human society, but much of the detail of this conceptual framework is filled in by his historical studies on the significance of 'court society' and one particular long-term social process around which Elias felt others tended to be organized: the civilizing process. Indeed, he developed and elaborated his theoretical position primarily through these studies, to which we turn in the next chapter.

4

ON CIVILIZING PROCESSES

The genesis and development of the modern, bourgeois, Western world is a problem which every major sociologist has addressed in one way or another. This is primarily because a grasp of its 'rules of formation' and its 'laws of movement' both helps us better understand the operation of the social world we live in, and also offers the possibility, at least, of gaining some sense of its potential future direction. Elias's approach to the origins of contemporary Western societies was rooted in dual synthesis of Freud with Marx on the one hand, and with Weber on the other. He drew on Marx's materialism to explain the development of a particular personality structure, emphasizing its 'production' by particular sets of social relations, and elaborated on Freud's understanding of the effects of developing civilization on psychic life in terms of Weber's conception of the state as organized around a monopoly of the means of violence. Elias's historicization of human psychology provides empirical support for an understanding of the processes by which changes in social relations are interwoven with changes in psychic structure. There are three 'nodes' to Elias's thinking on what he regarded as perhaps the most important social processes of all, 'civilizing' processes: *The Court Society* (originally 1933), *The Civilizing Process* (1939), and the gathering together of his major conceptual developments since the 1950s, *The Germans* (1996).

COURT SOCIETY

Elias's first major sociological work was *The Court Society*, completed in 1933 as his *Habilitationsschrift* under Karl Mannheim. It was the foundation upon which Elias's work on *The Civilizing Process* was built, although it was published much later: in 1969 in German and 1983 in English. The addition of a new preface, new sections and some reworking of the original text also often creates the impression that it was a later publication. There are three aspects of Elias's initial analysis of court society which are of particular significance:

1 his argument for identifying royal and aristocratic courts as key social units which played a vital role in the emergence of bourgeois, capitalist societies;
2 the analysis of a 'courtly rationality' which both preceded instrumental–legal rationality and continues as an under-current to it; and
3 the identification, in the dynamics of social relations in court society, of particular mechanisms of power and social differentiation which continue to operate in contemporary social life.

Here I will be concentrating on those aspects of the book which precede and underlie the subsequent development of Elias's ideas.

In sociology and history we are used to approaching the development of Western society from the Middle Ages onwards with a particular list of concepts capturing specific kinds of social units or collective entities. This list would include the city, the factory, the monastery, the state, bureaucratic or patrimonial organizations, feudal or capitalist economic structures, the family, Protestantism, the bourgeoisie, the working class and so on. *The Court Society* extends our understanding of the development of Western societies by identifying the *aristocracy* and the *courts* which emerged and developed from the Middle Ages onwards as far more than an outmoded form of ostentatious consumption, destined for the historical scrap heap and merely what was left behind in the transition to bourgeois society. Court society was, Elias argued, a historically significant form of social organization, with a dual relationship to the bourgeois society which followed it. On the one hand, bourgeois morality and forms of life were developed precisely in opposition to those of the courts: particularly the distinction between public and private life, the organization of life around criteria of instrumental, economic rationality, and the placement of a dedication to work at the centre of human existence. On the other hand, Elias saw that many features of the forms of social relations in court society also continued into bourgeois society, so that an understanding of court society would also illuminate many aspects of contemporary social relations which are less visible to us precisely because we believe we have left the world of *Dangerous Liaisons* in the past. 'By studying the structure of court society and seeking to understand one of the last great non-bourgeois figurations of the West,' argued Elias, 'we indirectly gain increased understanding of our own professional-bourgeois, urban-industrial society.'[1]

It was the royal and princely courts, suggested Elias, not the towns or cities, which had come to constitute the social nucleus of seventeenth-century European societies, and 'the town, as was said in the *ancien régime*, merely "aped" the court'.[2] Elias remarked on Weber's neglect of the court, arising from his concentration on the transition from patrimonial to legal-rational bureaucracies.[3] Most importantly, Elias felt that it was the court which established a particular mode of conduct and psychic structure, a certain habitus, which the bourgeois habitus was based on even as it differentiated itself from it. As he put it, 'aristocratic court society developed a civilizing and cultural physiognomy which was taken over by professional-bourgeois society partly as a heritage and partly as an antithesis and, preserved in this way, was further developed'.[4] Whereas Marx looked for the formation of modern social relations and a corresponding personality structure in the logic of the capitalist production process, Weber in Protestantism and bureaucracy, and Foucault in a range of social institutions and systems of knowledge about human beings, Elias argued that the extension of the familial households of French kings and their dependents into a larger 'court society' was a crucial foundation stone of contemporary psychic structure and social relations.

This argument is worked out, first, in the identification and analysis of 'courtly rationality' as a precursor to, and foundation for, the legal-rational bourgeois rationality on which Weber concentrated. For Elias 'rationality' at the most general level refers to the balance struck between short-term desires and emotional needs, and the longer-term consequences of human action. The more the balance is weighted towards the latter, the more human behaviour can be regarded as 'rational', although he added the qualification that emotional control can also go too far, since emotions and feelings have their own place in human relations and resist complete elimination.[5]

However, what constitutes being oriented to reality 'varies with the structure of social reality itself', which means that there are differing forms of 'rationality'. In comparing the rationality of court society with that of the professional bourgeoisie, Elias pointed out that while they both display 'a preponderance of long-term reality-oriented considerations over momentary affects',[6] among the bourgeoisie it is 'the calculation of financial gains and losses' which plays a leading role. In other words, the means of exercising power revolves around the acquisition of predominantly *economic* capital, and what constitutes rationality is organized around that concern. In court society, in contrast, power revolves around the acquisition of *symbolic* capital, status and prestige, which will often entail the generation of financial losses. As Elias put it:

> Bourgeois-industrial rationality is generated by the compulsion of the economic mesh; by it power-opportunities founded on private or public capital are made calculable. Court rationality is generated by the compulsion of the elite social mesh; by it people and prestige are made calculable as instruments of power.[7]

Behaviour which the Protestant bourgeoisie would regard as 'irrational' and 'unrealistic', made famous by Veblen's concept of 'conspicuous consumption', was exactly what was demanded by court society of all its members in order to function within its relations of power. In court society, individual existence and identity were profoundly *representational* – they consisted of how one exhibited one's position and status to everyone else, and this process of exhibition and performance was highly competitive and constantly fluctuating. It was a living embodiment of the symbolic interactionist argument that when something is defined as real, it is real in its consequences: court society was organized around this principle, making the struggles around definitions and representations of position, status and prestige the focus of all social relationships.

The main vehicle of the representation of social identity was the practices of etiquette and manners, because the rituals of etiquette both *demonstrated* each individual's position within the social network, and were the *means* by which individuals could negotiate and manoeuvre that position. The management of emotions was crucial to these manoeuvres, and advantage accrued to those who could control their emotions most effectively. As Elias put it:

> affective outbursts are difficult to control and calculate. They reveal the true feelings of the person concerned to a degree

that, because not calculated, can be damaging; they hand over trump cards to rivals for favour and prestige. Above all, they are a sign of weakness; and that is the position the court person fears most of all. *In this way the competition of court life enforces a curbing of the affects in favour of calculating and finely shaded behaviour in dealing with people.*[8]

This meant that there was no real division between public and private life – one's public position was heavily dependent on all aspects of one's relation with others, not merely behaviour confined to an as-yet non-existent 'public' realm. Unlike the world of the professional bourgeoisie, social effectivity 'was not decided in the professional sphere, then influencing private life, but behaviour at any time and every day could decide a person's place in society, could mean social success or failure', and 'society encompassed the whole being of its members'.[9] In bourgeois society, on the other hand, it was in the world of work where the main social constraints were concentrated, and a sphere of private life was carved out which, in principle at least, was meant to be no longer relevant to one's occupational or professional status. Weber's argument about the supposed 'impersonal' character of bureaucracy is a useful example here.

There were also 'counter-movements' within court society, 'attempts to emancipate "feeling", which are always at the same time attempts to emancipate the individual from social pressure',[10] but overtly at least in seventeenth-century France they usually failed. In court society there was, therefore, a tension between a principle of 'authenticity' and one of 'rationality', between the free expression of one's true emotional character and its management in the calculated pursuit of long-term ends, such as the maximization of power and prestige. The former was usually 'punished by social downfall or at least degradation'[11] in court society, and it was only once a boundary was established in bourgeois society between private and public life that there was a move towards a corresponding freeing of a realm of emotional authenticity from the competitive manoeuvrings for prestige, power and status, in turn confined to the public world of work, organizational life, and professional relationships.

The operation of this type of power relationship demanded continuous *observation* of both others and one's self, and the constantly fluctuating relations between various members of court society. Indeed, Elias regarded the form of observation in the court, its 'gaze', as similar to a sociological perspective, 'because it never attempts to consider the individual person in isolation, as a being deriving his essential regularities and characteristics from within. Rather, the individual is always observed in court society in his social context, as a *person in relation to others*.'[12] Monastic self-observation, which Weber and Foucault focused on, also aimed at disciplining and regulating emotional life, but Elias argued that court society promoted a 'specific form of self-observation', one with 'a view to self-discipline in *social life*',[13] essentially *complementary* to the observation of others. The point of observing others was to ascertain their true motives and desires, but also, more importantly, to search for any point of leverage to gain some advantage over them. The superiority of one's position was heavily dependent on how one displayed that superiority to subordinates. Elias cites Jean de La Bruyère in this regard: 'Let a favourite observe himself very closely; for if he keeps me waiting less than usual in his antechamber, if his face is more open, less frowning, if he listens to me more willingly or accompanies me farther to the door, I shall think he is beginning to fall and I shall be right'.[14] Authenticity was to be avoided at all costs, for it simply gave competitors advantages in the constant struggle for psychological dominance. La Bruyère again: 'A man who knows the court is master of his gestures, of his eyes and of his face; he is profound, impenetrable; he dissimulates bad offices, smiles at his enemies, controls his irritation, disguises his passions, belies his heart, speaks and acts against his feelings.'[15]

The second set of characteristics specific to court society concerned the mechanisms by which power relations operated. In the first place, its representational character meant that power relations were profoundly relational, characterized by a fundamental interdependence. Social superiority was heavily dependent on the extent to which others recognized it, and unless one was in a structurally central position, such as the king, it disappeared when that recognition evaporated. The nobility needed the king 'because within this social field only life at his court gave them access to the economic opportunities and prestige that enabled them to live as a nobility'.[16] However, the king also needed the nobility as a basis for a collective culture, as a buffer zone dividing off the rest of the population, but 'above all as an indispensable weight in the equilibrium of classes that he ruled'.[17] The king's superiority lay in the fact that 'each individual noble depended on the king far more than the king depended on each individual noble', and 'there was always a "reserve army" of nobles from which he could pick a replacement'.[18] As a *collective* entity the nobility could usurp the king, but their competition with each other constantly undermined such a possibility, to the advantage of the central actor managing the tensions among them, the king, who would assist this or that group in their competition with one another. 'The king,' wrote Elias, 'appeared over and again as the ally and helper of each class or corporation against the threats from other groups which they could not master on their own.'[19] But even Louis XIV, the Sun King, 'proves on closer scrutiny to be an individual who was enmeshed . . . in a specific network of interdependencies'. The power of kings was not a possession which simply lay 'in' themselves, for they could preserve their power 'only by a carefully calculated strategy which was governed by the peculiar structure of court society in the narrow sense, and more broadly by society at large'.[20]

The driving forces were *competition*, and the *opportunities* for *advantage* which competitive success offered to its participants.

Court society 'was shot through with the countless rivalries of people trying to preserve their position by marking it off from those below while at the same time improving it by reducing the demarcation from those above'.[21] The '*formula of need*' which underlay the operation and reproduction of the court figuration was the fact that 'it offered the people forming it satisfaction of the various needs that were constantly reproduced in them'.[22] It was the competition between various social groups for advantages over others which generated both the willingness to submit to the demands of etiquette and the process of 'courtization', where the body, emotions and desires were increasingly subjected to stringent controls and ever more demanding forms of self-discipline. Competition also drove the spread of many aspects of courtly rationality first to the higher bourgeois strata, in their attempts to enter court society, and then in turn to the strata below them.

Bourgeois rationality was distinct from courtly rationality, largely through the establishment of a clearer opposition between public and private life, an organization of the definition of self-worth around the world of work, and a prioritization of economic acquisition. However, Elias's analysis of court society reveals more than the prehistory of bourgeois society, it also reveals a deeper layer of social relations which continues to the present day. The organization of power relations around the representation of social prestige still plays an important role in contemporary societies, despite the lack of fit with our self-image as instrumentally rational moderns. Much of the dynamics of court society can still be seen in the day-to-day workings of any modern organization, and success in contemporary social life may be more dependent on adept display, performance and representation than we are usually willing to admit. As Elias put it:

> Despite their formal organizational framework based on written contracts and documents, which was developed only

in rudimentary form in the state of Louis XIV, there are in many organizations of our time, even industrial and commercial ones, rivalries for status, fluctuations in the balance between groups, exploitation of internal rivalries by superiors, and other phenomena that have emerged in the study of court society. But as the main regulation of human relationships in large organizations is formalized in a highly impersonal manner, such phenomena usually have a more or less unofficial and informal character today. In court society we therefore find quite openly and on a large scale many phenomena that exist below the surface of highly bureaucratized organizations.[23]

The roots of informal organizational structures and organizational culture can, therefore, be seen to have originated in the dynamics of court society, continuing an older form of rationality beneath the surface of the instrumental–legal rationality around which modern organizations are supposed to revolve. Exactly how these two types of rationality related to each other, how their emergence could be placed within broader historical processes, and what the significance of the forms of conduct developed in court society would have for the rest of the population in European societies, were the questions that Elias turned to when he arrived in Paris and then London, and began work on *Über den Prozeß der Zivilisation.*

PROCESSES OF CIVILIZATION

'Civilization' is a concept we normally use with some caution, especially in social science, partly because we no longer wish to admit explicitly to the opposition with 'barbarism'. It is far more common to speak of 'modern', 'Western', 'industrial', or 'capitalist' societies. Nonetheless, it is conceivable that the members of every culture see themselves as more 'civilized' than some others, and that the very basis of any culture's group identity is the opposition between all the positive virtues of its 'civilization' and the 'barbarism' of other, lesser cultures. The long-running tension between Christianity and Islam is only one example among many. What Elias felt sure was the product of a long historical process had, by the end of the eighteenth century, come to be defined by Europeans 'simply as an expression of their own higher gifts'.[24] It became a crucial part of Europeans' sense of superiority over all other peoples in the world: 'the consciousness of their own superiority, the consciousness of this "civilization", from now on serves at least those nations which have become colonial conquerors, and therefore a kind of upper class to large sections of the non-European world, as a justification of their rule'.[25] It was Europeans' perception of themselves as particularly 'civilized', at the very hour of their indulgence in a horrific barbarism, around which Elias organized his observations about the development of modern social life, because he felt it went to the heart of the constitution of the psychic structure characteristic of contemporary European societies.

Elias had a dual concern in *The Civilizing Process*: first, to demonstrate that 'we can never understand the relation between the social process and the "psychical" as long as we see in the psychical only something static and unchangeable, as long as we do not also see the psychical as "in process"'[26] and, second, 'to investigate, step by step, which social processes are the motors of this psychical change'.[27] He suggested that what we experience as 'civilization' is founded on a particular habitus, a particular psychic structure which has changed over time, and which can only be understood in connection with changes in the forms taken by broader social relationships. Referring to Morris Ginsberg's discussion of the 'plasticity' of human nature, Elias insisted that 'the molding of instinctual life, including its compulsive features, is a function of social interdependencies that persist throughout life', and these interdependencies change as the structure of society changes. 'To the variation in this structure correspond,' wrote Elias, 'the differences in personality structure that can be observed in history.'[28] The first point was explored by Elias in relation to the successive editions of a variety of etiquette manuals, beginning with Erasmus' (1530) tract *De civilitate morum puerilium* (On civility in children), and the second in relation to the history of state formation in Britain, France and Germany, particularly the gradual monopolization of the means of violence by the state.

The first volume of *The Civilizing Process* identifies gradual changes in expectations of people's interpersonal conduct in European societies, as well as the way they approached their own bodily functions and emotions. Elias began his story in the Middle Ages, not because he felt it marked any particular origin or 'as has sometime been asserted, the stage of "barbarism" or "primitiveness"',[29] but largely in order to have a story to tell, saying that 'the medieval standard must suffice as a starting point, without itself being closely examined, so that the movement, the developmental curve joining it to the modern age may be pursued'.[30] In outlining 'correct' behaviour, Erasmus' book indicated 'attitudes that we have lost, that some among us would perhaps call "barbaric" or "uncivilized"', and it spoke 'of many things that have in the meantime become unspeakable, and of many others that are now taken for granted'.[31] Following Huizinga's[32] account, Elias suggested that typical medieval conduct was characterized by 'its simplicity, its naïvete', emotions were 'expressed more violently and directly' and there were 'fewer psychological nuances and complexities in the general stock of ideas'.[33]

Elias found that as time went on the standards applied to violence, sexual behaviour, bodily functions, eating habits, table manners and forms of speech became gradually more sophisticated, with an increasing threshold of shame, embarrassment and repugnance. In medieval society,

> Compared to later eras, social control is mild. Manners, measured against later ones, are relaxed in all senses of the

word. One ought not to snort or smack one's lips while eating. One ought not to spit across the table or blow one's nose on the tablecloth (for this is used for wiping greasy fingers) or into the fingers (with which one holds the common dish). Eating from the same dish or plate as others is taken for granted. One must only refrain from falling on the dish like a pig, and from dipping bitten food into the communal sauce.[34]

Gradually more and more aspects of human behaviour become regarded as 'distasteful', and 'the distasteful is *removed behind the scenes of social life*'.

Again and again, wrote Elias, we see 'how characteristic is this movement of segregation, this hiding "behind the scenes" of what has become distasteful'.[35] For example, a French etiquette manual from 1729 advises its readers as follows:

It is very impolite to keep poking your finger into your nostrils, and still more insupportable to put what you have pulled from your nose into your mouth. . . .

You should avoid making a noise when blowing your nose . . . before blowing it, it is impolite to spend a long time taking out your handkerchief. *It shows a lack of respect toward the people you are with* to unfold it in different places to see where you are to use it. You should take your handkerchief from your pocket and use it quickly in such a way that you are scarcely noticed by others.

After blowing your nose you should take care not to look into your handkerchief. It is correct to fold it immediately and replace it in your pocket.[36]

One of the indications of the fact that some process of 'civilization' has taken place is, Elias felt, our feelings of unease when hearing of the behaviour which Erasmus described, and our sense of what is 'barbaric' or 'uncivilized' is expressed in 'the greater or lesser discomfort we feel towards people who discuss or mention their bodily functions more openly, who conceal and restrain these functions less than we do'.[37] 'Formerly,' suggested another etiquette manual in 1672, 'one was allowed to take from one's mouth what one could not eat and drop it on the floor, providing it was done skilfully. Now that would be very disgusting.'[38]

Elias described medieval society as being characterized generally by 'a lesser degree of social control and constraint of instinctual life',[39] particularly by a *violence* which dominated everyday life and was rarely subject to much social or self-control. His interpretation of his evidence was that it suggested 'unimaginable emotional outbursts in which – with rare exceptions – everyone who is able abandons himself to the extreme pleasures of ferocity, murder, torture, destruction, and sadism'.[40] The general behaviour of medieval knights was captured with the example of Bernard de Cazenac, who spent his days plundering churches, attacking pilgrims, oppressing widows and orphans, and taking pleasure in 'mutilating the innocent', as well as that of his wife, who had women's 'breasts hacked off or their nails torn off'.[41] Elias felt that there was great pleasure in killing and torturing, describing it as 'a socially permitted pleasure'; indeed, to some degree 'the social structure even pushed its members in this direction, making it seem necessary and practically advantageous to behave in this way'.[42]

The social process of 'courtization' subjected first knights and warriors, and then ever-expanding circles of the population,[43] to an increasing demand that such expressions of violence be regulated, that emotions and impulses be placed more firmly in the service of the long-term requirements of complex networks of social interaction. Slowly and gradually, argued Elias, 'the code of behaviour becomes stricter and the degree of consideration expected of others becomes greater,' and 'the social imperative not to offend others becomes more binding'.[44] In court society we see the beginnings of a form of mutual and self-observation which Elias referred to as a 'psychological' form of perception.

> The new stage of courtesy and its representation, summed up in the concept of *civilité*, is very closely bound up with this manner of seeing, and gradually becomes more so. In order to be really 'courteous' by the standards of *civilité*, one is to some extent obliged to observe, to look about oneself and pay attention to people and their motives. . . . The increasing tendency of people to observe themselves and others is one sign of how the whole question of behaviour is now taking on a different character: people mold themselves and others more deliberately than in the Middle Ages.[45]

Elias did not see courts as the 'cause' or driving force of this process, but as its *nucleus*, and he drew a parallel with the form taken by a chemical process like crystallization, 'in which a liquid . . . [being] subjected to conditions of chemical change . . . first takes on crystalline form at a small nucleus, while the rest then gradually crystallizes around this core'. However, 'nothing would be more erroneous than to take the core of crystallization for the cause of the transformation'.[46]

The result was a particular kind of habitus or 'second nature', an 'automatic self-restraint, a habit that, within certain limits, also functions when a person is alone'.[47] Elias argued that the restraint imposed by increasingly differentiated and complex networks of social relations became increasingly internalized, and less dependent on its maintenance by external social institutions, developing what Freud was to recognize as a superego. Referring to the example of sexual impulses, Elias wrote that they were:

> slowly but progressively suppressed from the public life of society. . . . And this restraint, like all others, is enforced less and less by direct physical force. It is cultivated in the individual from an early age as habitual self-restraint by the structure of social life, by the pressure of social institutions in general, and by certain executive organs of society (above all, the family) in particular. Thereby the social commands and prohibitions

become increasingly a part of the self, a strictly regulated super-ego.[48]

He cautions, too, against seeing a more recent relaxation of moral codes and restrictions as indicating any reversal of the overall process of civilization. For example, Elias felt that increasingly daring bathing costumes and less overt restrictions on speaking about sexual matters and bodily functions were only possible 'in a society in which a high degree of restraint is taken for granted', so that both women and men are 'absolutely sure that each individual is curbed by self-control and a strict code of etiquette', constituting 'a relaxation which remains within the framework of a particular "civilized" standard of behaviour involving a very high degree of automatic constraint and affect-transformation, conditioned to become a habit'.[49]

He did say that these developments in habitus were not unilinear, that 'the civilizing process does not follow a straight line' and that 'on a smaller scale there are the most diverse criss-cross movements, shifts and spurts in this or that direction'.[50] Nonetheless, at this point he felt that there was a more significant overall tendency with a particular direction, towards increasing 'regulation of the affects in the form of self-control'.[51] 'Regardless,' then, 'of how much the tendencies may criss-cross, advance and recede, relax or tighten on a small scale, the direction of the main movement – as far as is visible up to now – is the same for all kinds of behaviour.'[52]

Elias always asserted that these changes were only comprehensible within developing patterns of social relations and changing social figurations, and it was to the explanation of the transformation of psychic structure revealed by the etiquette books and other historical evidence that he turned in the second volume of The Civilizing Process. 'When enquiring into social processes,' he wrote, 'one must look at the web of human relationships, at society itself, to find the compulsions that keep them in motion, and give them their particular form and their particular direction.'[53] Of those changes in the 'web of human relationships', Elias regarded two as especially significant. First, there was 'the process of state-formation, and within it the advancing centralization of society',[54] especially as it was expressed in the absolutist states of seventeenth- and eighteenth-century Europe. Second, he stressed the gradual differentiation of society, the increasing range, diversity and interdependence of competing social positions and functions composing European societies. There were other, related changes which he also mentioned, such as the development of a money economy and urbanization, but it was these two processes of social development on which he placed most emphasis. In Elias's words:

> What lends the civilizing process in the West its special and unique character is the fact that here the division of functions has attained a level, the monopolies of force and taxation a solidity, and interdependence and competition an extent, both in terms of physical space and of numbers of people involved, unequalled in world history.[55]

There was, Elias believed, a powerful 'logic' built into any configuration of competing social units, such as states, towns or communities, towards an increasing monopolization of power and, correspondingly, of the means of violence. He saw this 'logic' as emerging from the dynamics of social, political and economic competition, and saw it as being organized around two 'mechanisms': the 'monopoly mechanism', which 'once set in motion, proceeds like clockwork',[56] and the 'royal mechanism'. The operation of the 'monopoly mechanism' was summarized as follows:

> in a major social unit . . . a large number of the smaller social units which, through their interdependence, constitute the larger one, are of roughly equal social power and are thus able

to compete freely – unhampered by pre-existing monopolies – for the means to social power, i.e. primarily the means of subsistence and production, the probability is high that some will be victorious and others vanquished, and that gradually, as a result, fewer and fewer will control more and more opportunities, and more and more units will be eliminated from the competition, becoming directly or indirectly dependent on an ever-decreasing number.[57]

Unless some countervailing process is set in motion, argued Elias, competition would generally drive any human figuration towards 'a state in which all opportunities are controlled by a single authority: a system with open opportunities has become a system with closed opportunities'.[58]

Elias argued that accompanying the monopoly mechanism was another tendency, that of what he called the 'royal mechanism', which was a feature of the *evenness* or *indecisiveness* of any pattern of competition. If social conditions are not bad enough for any one group to risk the loss of their current position, and power is distributed so evenly that every group is fearful of any other group gaining the slightest advantage, 'they tie each other's hands' and 'this gives the central authority better chances than any other constellation within society'.[59] The general principle of the 'royal mechanism' is thus:

the hour of the strong central authority within a highly differentiated society strikes when the ambivalence of interests of the most important functional groups grows so large, and power is distributed so evenly between them, that there can be neither a decisive compromise nor a decisive conflict between them.[60]

The position of a central authority is, then, not based simply on some greater power that they might have over any other social unit, but on their function as a mediator or nodal point for the conflicts between the other groups in society, which can neither individually overcome any of the others, nor stop competing to the degree required to form an effective alliance with each other.

The consequence of these mechanisms in terms of power relations was not, however, simply to increase the power chances of those individuals and groups in more central positions of authority and influence, which is how we usually think of any process of monopolization. Elias emphasized that 'the more people are made dependent by the monopoly mechanism, the greater becomes the power of the dependent, not only individually but also collectively, in relation to the one or more monopolists'. This was because those in the more central, monopoly positions were also made increasingly dependent on 'ever more dependents in preserving and exploiting the power potential they have monopolized'.[61] The greater monopolization of power chances is thus accompanied by a greater *collective* democratization, at least, because a monopoly position is itself dependent on a larger and more complex network of social groups and units. A useful example here would be the position of the head of government in any of the advanced industrial countries.

It was the 'monopoly mechanism' and the 'royal mechanism', felt Elias, which lay at the heart of the state-formation process in Europe, which was in turn necessarily accompanied by an increasing monopolization of the means of violence, and a pressure towards other means of exercising power in social relations. Rather than the use of violence, social 'success' is more and more dependent on 'continuous reflection, foresight, and calculation, self-control, precise and articulate regulation of one's own affects, knowledge of the whole terrain, human and non-human, in which one acts'.[62]

Elias argued that this 'rationalization' of human conduct, its placement at the service of long-term goals and the increasing internalization of social constraint was closely tied to the process of state formation and development of monopolies of physical force:

The peculiar stability of the apparatus of mental self-restraint which emerges as a decisive trait built into the habitus of every 'civilized' human being, stands in the closest relationship to the monopolization of physical force and the growing stability of the central organs of society. Only with the formation of this kind of relatively stable monopolies do societies acquire those characteristics as a result of which the individuals forming them get attuned, from infancy, to a highly regulated and differentiated pattern of self-restraint; only in conjunction with these monopolies does this kind of self-restraint require a higher degree of automaticity, does it become, as it were, 'second nature'.[63]

The 'requirement' placed on each individual is not a direct one, but one mediated by one's own reflection on the consequences of differing patterns of behaviour. 'The actual compulsion', suggested Elias, 'is one that the individual exerts on himself either as a result of his knowledge of the possible consequences of his moves in the game in intertwining activities, or as a result of corresponding gestures of adults which have helped to pattern his own behaviour as a child'.[64]

Underlying the processes of state-formation and nation-building were, second, others of increasing social *differentiation*, increasing density, complexity, and what Elias called 'lengthening chains of social interdependence'. In his words:

The closer the web of interdependencies becomes in which the individual is enmeshed with the advancing division of functions, the larger the social spaces over which this network extends and which become integrated into functional or institutional units – the more threatened is the social existence of the individual who gives way to spontaneous impulses and emotions, the greater is the social advantage of those able to moderate their affects, and the more strongly is each individual constrained from an early age to take account of the effects of

> his own or other people's actions on a whole series of links in
> the social chain.[65]

A central developmental process in European societies was their
increasing density, produced by a combination of population
growth and urbanization, and the ever-larger circles of people that
any single individual would be interdependent with, no matter
how fleetingly.

He spoke of the 'conveyor belts' running through individuals'
lives growing 'longer and more complex',[66] requiring us to 'attune'
our conduct to the actions of others,[67] and becoming the dominant influence on our existence, so that we are less 'prisoners of our
passions' and more captive to the requirements of an increasingly
complex 'web of actions',[68] particularly a demand for 'constant
hindsight and foresight in interpreting the actions and intentions
of others'.[69] Just as important as the 'length' of chains of interdependence was the increasing *ambivalence* of overlapping and
multiple networks: as social relations become more complex and
contradictory, the same people or groups could be 'friends, allies or
partners' in one context and 'opponents, competitors or enemies'
in another. 'This fundamental ambivalence of interests', wrote
Elias, is 'one of the most important structural characteristics
of more highly developed societies, and a chief factor moulding
civilized conduct.'[70]

Elias saw human conduct as subject to a variety of civilizing
processes, all of which 'tend to produce a transformation of the
whole drive and affect economy in the direction of a more
continuous, stable and even regulation of drives and affects in
all areas of conduct, in all sectors of his life'.[71] The growing
interdependence produced by increasingly intense social differentiation, as well as the monopolization of violence by the state,
meant that:

> a social apparatus is established in which the constraints
> between people are lastingly transformed into self-constraints.

> These self-constraints, a function of the perpetual hindsight and foresight instilled in the individual from childhood in accordance with his integration in extensive chains of action, have partly the form of conscious self-control and partly that of automatic habit.[72]

We are all compelled more and more to regulate our conduct 'in an increasingly differentiated, more even and more stable manner'. Reiterating his formulations in *The Court Society*, Elias referred to this increasing self-regulation as a process of 'psychologization' and 'rationalization', because it revolved around the growing reflexive understanding of our own actions, those of others, their interrelationships and their consequences. The effect of this on our habitus is that:

> the more complex and stable control of conduct is increasingly instilled in the individual from his earliest years as an automatism, a self-compulsion that he cannot resist even if he consciously wishes to. The web of actions grows so complex and extensive, the effort required to behave 'correctly' within it becomes so great, that beside the individual's conscious self-control an automatic, blindly functioning apparatus of self-control is firmly established.[73]

Later he described the internalization of a disciplined sense of *time* as a 'paradigmatic'[74] example of this establishment of an automatic apparatus of self-regulation.[75] Although there may be counter-movements, periods of more uneven development and variations between countries and regions, 'the general direction of the change in conduct, the "trend" of the movement in civilization, is everywhere the same'. The development of habitus 'always veers towards a more or less automatic self-control, to the subordination of short-term impulses to the commands of an imagined longer-term view, and to the formation of a more complex and secure "superego" agency'.[76] The dynamics of this development, Elias felt, was also always the same in Western societies, beginning with 'small leading groups' and then affecting 'broader and broader strata',[77] not through some process of 'diffusion', but resulting from the dynamics of social competition.

There were, finally, three important qualifications which Elias had to repeat on a number of occasions in response to his critics. First, he maintained that his concept of a civilizing process in European social history did not imply the existence of any sort of original 'state of nature' in some early historical period. There is 'no zero point in the historicity of human development',[78] no example of human existence in which there were no social constraints built into the development of all human individuals from infancy to whatever their society regarded as adulthood. Second, he also suggested that there was no particular *beginning* to the civilizing process, so that in any given period people will regard themselves as more civilized than the peoples in the preceding periods. 'Wherever we start,' he wrote, 'there is movement, something that went before.'[79] Third, he also felt that civilizing processes were *never-ending*, and that we can never regard ourselves as having attained a state of 'true' civilization, certainly not in contemporary societies. Unlike Marx, then, he did not anticipate an 'end' to history. Although he was confident that considerable social development had taken place since antiquity, he was equally sure that we had by no means stopped 'civilizing' ourselves and each other, which was why the final line in *The Civilizing Process* included these words from Holbach: 'la civilisation . . . n'est pas encore terminée'.[80] Later he said: 'The civilization of which I speak is never completed and always endangered.'[81]

The Civilizing Process was completed in 1939, and both Elias himself and his interpreters, supportive as well as critical, have tended towards the view that his understanding of the development and dynamics of Western societies did not change substantially afterwards. The development of Elias's ideas between the 1960s and 1980s reveals, however, a more nuanced picture, and his writings can be regarded as ranging from a reiteration of his arguments in *The Court Society* and *The Civilizing Process*, through a development or refinement of his ideas, to a distinct change of direction and emphasis. How his later thoughts were spread along this continuum is the topic of the next section.

THE GERMANS

There are four major themes running through *The Germans*: first, the question of the historical formation of national identity, with specific reference to Germany, and how processes of both civilization and decivilization interrelate within the development of any particular nation–state and the habitus of its members. The second, related theme is the contradictory and ambivalent character of processes of civilization, their 'dark' sides and the question of 'civilized barbarism'. The third is the process of 'informalization', developing a point made in *The Civilizing Process* concerning how increased self-restraint can manifest itself in an apparent relaxation of norms surrounding a variety of human activities. Finally, Elias drew attention to the significance of what Mannheim referred to as 'the problem of generations', the structure and distribution of opportunities and power between the established generation and the next, and the role that this can play in explaining a range of social and political events such as the youth rebellions of the 1960s and, more particularly, German terrorism in the 1960s and 1970s.

In *The Civilizing Process* Elias's primary focus was on the characteristics of social development which Western European societies shared with each other, rather than the features of the history of particular nation–states which distinguished them from one another. This does not mean that he neglected relations and differences between states; *The Civilizing Process* begins with a discussion of differences between French and German perspectives on culture and civilization, and his analysis of European state formation was organized around the specific developments in France, Germany and England, all 'social formations with a quite specific structure and a momentum and regularity of their own'.[82] Nonetheless, his eye was ultimately on the ways in which the state formation processes in different countries were converging, on the formation of ever-larger 'survival units' and monopolies of violence, on the similar effects of lengthening chains of inter-dependence. Indeed, the very distinctiveness of Elias's approach lies to a large extent in his emphasis on the dynamics of the larger *network* of nation–states in understanding the development of any single nation, anticipating more recent discussions of the world economic system and processes of 'globalization'.[83] In relation to national economies, he argued that:

> we should not look at one industrial nation on its own if we wish to gain a clear picture of the nature and strength of the relationships of pressure and tension within it. For the level of the living standard ... is always partly determined by the position of the whole society in the global network of different nation–states and empires with its further division of functions.[84]

He used the category 'nation' sparingly, and his analysis of the civilizing process emphasized tendencies which all the Western nations had in common with each other, such as increasing social differentiation and interdependence. The subtitle of *Über den Prozeß der Zivilisation* referred to 'changes in the behaviour of secular upper classes in the Occident'. It is thus fair to remark, as Johan Arnason does, that Elias's earlier work 'contains no distinctive interpretation of the nation as a pattern of collective identity or of nationalism as a socio-cultural current'.[85]

It is also true to say that Elias's ideas changed after the 1950s to give more attention to the specificity of historical development within particular nation–states, as well as on the features of relations between states. Hans Haferkamp has referred to this change of focus as 'a shift of emphasis from intra-societal to inter-state-societal processes',[86] a shift which is also reflected in the change in terminology from *the* civilizing process to civilizing process*es*. The particular expression of this change in orientation is his analysis of the 'peculiarities of the Germans' which underlay the rise of fascism and the Holocaust. His emphasis in *The Civilizing Process* had been on identifying the 'long-term trend' which would eventually override the changes in the direction of the civilizing process, but in analysing the rise of Hitler and the Nazi state's genocidal practices it was clear that the reality of 'decivilization' needed to be taken far more seriously, as many of his critics had argued. Elias thus described his analysis in *The Germans* as 'an attempt to tease out the developments in the German national habitus which made possible the decivilizing spurt of the Hitler epoch, and to work out the connections between them and the long-term process of state-formation in Germany'.[87]

The aggression and violence which took place under Hitler, suggested Elias, could be explained in terms of four peculiarities of the German state-formation process. The first was the particular position of the German territories within a larger figuration of nation–states, caught in particular between the Slavs in the East and the Franks in the West. The second was the relative weakness of the German territories in comparison to surrounded states, and their exposure to foreign invasion, which, Elias argued, 'led to military bearing and warlike actions being highly regarded and often idealized'.[88] The third was the larger number of breaks and discontinuities in the development of the German state, and the fourth was the ideological weakness of the bourgeoisie relative to the military aristocracy. Elias argued that the aristocracy's greater success in unifying Germany 'led to an outcome which can perhaps be described as the capitulation of the broad circles of the middle class to the aristocracy'.[89] The 'central question' in analysing the 'civilized barbarism' of the Hitler period was, suggested Elias, 'how the fortunes of a nation over the centuries become sedimented into the habitus of its individual members'.[90]

Elias expressed contradictory views at different points on the time frame within which processes of decivilization might overwhelm those of civilization. In *The Civilizing Process* he declared that 'the armor of civilized conduct would crumble very rapidly if, through a change in society, the degree of insecurity that existed earlier were to break in upon us again, and if danger became as incalculable as it once was'.[91] However, in *The Germans*, and this is more consistent with his general perspective in *The Civilizing Process*, he argued that the emergence of brutalized and dehumanized behaviour within relatively civilized societies 'always requires considerable time', and argued that 'terror and horror hardly ever manifest themselves without a fairly long process in which conscience decomposes'.[92]

A central feature of the ideology and culture of industrializing state–societies in the nineteenth century, wrote Elias, was a fundamental tension between a valorization of the collective entity of the nation–state on the one hand, and human individuals on the other, between the demands of nationalism and the hopes and expectations of liberalism.[93] He suggested that 'the development of a dual and inherently contradictory code of norms is one of the common features of all countries which have undergone the transformation from an aristocratic–dynastic into a more democratic national state'.[94] Elias also felt that from the nineteenth century onwards – essentially from the beginnings of movements for political and social democracy[95] – nationalism came to play a crucial part in individual identity-formation, with the value attached to any individual's nation being central to their own perception of their personal self-worth. 'The image of a nation experienced by an individual who forms part of that nation', wrote Elias, 'is also constituent of that person's self-image.'[96]

National identity is thus a central source of personal meaning and value; indeed, of the social sources of worth, Elias thought that today 'nations in their relationship to one another, in their rank-order, appear to have become the dominant and most powerful of all these supra-individual influences on people's feelings of meaning and value'.[97] A useful example here is the emotional response to performances in the Olympic Games and the success or failure of 'our' athletes in that forum, a feature of the significance of sport which will be taken up in the next chapter.

In the case of Germany, Elias considered that the tenuousness and fragility of German state-formation generated a fearfulness and anxiety about national 'worth', which encouraged a tipping of the balance towards a commitment to the demands and authority of the collectivity as opposed to the expectations of a respect for individual self-worth. As Elias put it:

> the cumulative effect of Germany's disturbed history – a history marked in the long term by defeats and consequent power losses, and which gave rise correspondingly to a broken national pride, a national identity very uncertain of itself, a backwards-looking national ideal which involved the projection of a fantasy picture of the greater past into the future – facilitated the emergence of a particularly malignant variant of beliefs and behavioural tendencies which also arose elsewhere.[98]

The deeply rooted cultural dominance of the German military aristocracy generated a tolerance, indeed an expectation, of rule from above and little or no sense of the importance of democratic participation from the ruled.[99] Elias argued that 'the personality structure, conscience-formation and code of behaviour had all become attuned to this form of regime'.[100]

When an attempt was made to establish a liberal democratic state system in the Weimar Republic, then, it faced a range of significant obstacles rooted in the political culture and individual habitus of ordinary Germans, obstacles which essentially arose from an absence of many of the features of the civilizing process, since the movement away from political authoritarianism 'requires the learning of new social techniques and skills which make greater demands of people's independence and self-control and ability to make judgements of their own'.[101] The historical development of German society, argued Elias, 'often produced a rather weak individual conscience' which was 'dependent on someone outside watching and reinforcing the compulsion, the discipline which individuals were incapable of imposing unaided on themselves'.[102] In addition, the commitment to the maintenance of what was experienced as an unstable and fragile national identity encouraged a hostility towards 'outsiders' or 'foreigners' who appeared to threaten that national identity. All these processes combined both to produce genocidal behaviour among particular groups in German society and to undermine other Germans' ability to resist the forces of conformity and obedience to the dictates of the nation, the state, and their personification, the Führer.

The second important feature of Elias's thinking in *The Germans* was the attention he paid to the question of 'modern barbarism'. In *The Civilizing Process*, the relationship between barbarism and civilization had been presented largely as mutually exclusive, one turning into the other, with possible 'reversals' of direction. To a large extent *The Germans* is consistent with this line of argument, raising the possibility that specific processes of state-formation produce either a 'deficient' process of civilization, or result in a clear process of decivilization encouraging the more widespread manifestation of brutal and violent conduct. However, Elias also raised the possibility that civilization and decivilization can occur *simultaneously*. For example, he made the point that the monopolization of physical force by the state, through the military and the police, cuts in two directions and has a Janus-faced character,[103] because such monopolies of force can then be all the more effectively wielded by powerful groups within any given nation–state, as indeed they did under the Nazi regime. Pursuing a line of thought he had been developing since the 1970s,[104] in one of his entries to a German dictionary of sociology published in 1986 he argued for the reversibility of social processes, and suggested that 'shifts in one direction can make room for shifts in the opposite direction,' so that 'a dominant process directed at greater integration could go hand in hand with a partial disintegration'.[105] Similarly, in *The Germans* he remarked that the example of the Hitler regime showed 'not only that processes of growth and decay can go hand in hand but that the latter can also predominate relative to the former'.[106] In a critique of Kingsley Davis' understanding of social norms, he argued that Davis emphasized the integrative effect of norms at the expense of their 'dividing and excluding character'. Elias pointed out that social norms had an 'inherently double-edged character', since in the very process of binding some people together, they turn those people against others. Critics like Stefan Breuer, however, have remarked that a central problem with Elias's work overall is his disinclination to perceive processes of social integration as being accompanied by other, equally significant processes of social disintegration and decomposition,[107] and we will examine the extent to which remarks such as these by Elias deal with this apparently more pervasive feature of his work in the final section of this chapter.

Third, Elias developed a point he had made in *The Civilizing Process* concerning the effects of increasing self-restraint on the character of explicit rules and norms governing human behaviour. As social restraint becomes increasingly 'second nature' to individuals, social rules and sanctions become less significant and we can observe a more relaxed and informal attitude to manners and etiquette. He referred to a general relaxation of norms in the period after World War I, in relation to what is said about natural functions as well as 'modern bathing and dancing practices', and argued that this was:

only possible because the level of habitual, technically and institutionally consolidated self-control, the individual capacity to restrain one's urges and behaviour in correspondence with the more advanced feelings for what is offensive, has on the whole been secured. It is a relaxation within the framework of an already established standard.[108]

Elias introduced the concept of the 'informalization process' to capture this dimension of civilizing processes, although it was first used and developed by the Dutch sociologist Cas Wouters.[109] Using the example of sexual behaviour, Elias argued that a less authoritarian system of sexual norms actually increases the demands made on each individual to regulate their own behaviour, or suffer the consequences. Regarding intimate relationships, he said that:

the main burden of shaping life together . . . now lies on the shoulders of the individuals concerned. Thus informalization brings with it stronger demands on apparatuses of self-constraint, and, at the same time, frequent experimentation and structural insecurity; one cannot really follow existing models, one has to work out for oneself a dating strategy as well as a strategy for living together through a variety of ongoing experiments.[110]

Elias said the same of the more informal relations between superiors and subordinates in the workplace, which also requires a greater degree of self-restraint in the absence of formal, explicit rules and formulae governing everyday conduct.

As power relations change and the rules of human interaction become less formalized and routinized, more flexible, we are all compelled to develop a more self-reflexive and sophisticated apparatus of self-regulation to be able to negotiate such an ever-changing and contingent network of social relationships. The declining relevance of an established code of behaviour 'inevitably brings with it a widespread feeling of uncertainty to many people who are caught up in the turmoil of change'.[111] What we might perceive, then, as an increase in individual 'freedom' is actually a greater demand for self-compulsion and self-management. It is at this point where Elias's ideas link up with those of Foucault on 'governmentality' in liberal democracies,[112] and they suggest a re-thinking of his views on sexuality as being increasingly 'hidden behind the scenes' or 'constrained' – we will examine this question in the next section.

Fourth, Elias also drew attention to an issue which he had only touched on in *The Civilizing Process*, namely that processes of social change could only be properly understood in terms of a relation between *generations*, between dominant social groups growing older and gradually losing their dominance and rising younger groups striving to improve their position within the established power relations. Karl Mannheim had referred to this as 'The problem of generations' in an essay first published in 1928.[113] Mannheim's piece engaged in some important conceptual ground-clearing, making a variety of important points about how the social phenomenon of 'generations' emerges from the biological facts of ageing and physical reproduction, including how a variety of socially conditioned 'generation units' can exist within the same physical generation and the relationship between generational conflict and the rate of social change. Elias fleshed out and expanded on Mannheim's arguments in a comparison of the structural position of right-wing German youth groups in the 1920s and 1930s, and left–right terrorist groups in the 1960s and 1970s, both examples of outbreaks of organized violence within state–societies which had otherwise more or less monopolized the means of violence.

The central point around which Elias's arguments revolve is the idea that although any given younger generation strives for meaning and personal fulfilment as well as for opportunities and power, those opportunities can widen or narrow depending on particular historical configurations. He commented that 'it is easy to distinguish between periods with comparatively open channels for upward mobility for the younger generations, and other periods in which these channels become narrower and narrower and perhaps for a while even become completely blocked'.[114] More generally:

> The narrowing and widening of life chances, and opportunities for meaning in general and career chances in particular, for the younger generations of a society at any one time are processes that undoubtedly most strongly affect the balance of power between the generations. One could say that these processes form the kernel of social conflicts between the generations.[115]

Elias felt that although the processes of succession of generations can to some extent be managed by established older groups, the overall opportunity structure for rising generations was largely unplanned and resistant to conscious control. For example, periods of peace are in fact times when 'the circulation of generations becomes more sluggish',[116] whereas periods of war tend to open up new opportunities for the younger generation. Indeed, Elias suggested that one of the bases of Hitler's success among young Germans was the fact that his particular mobilization of the nationalist ideology of the German *Volk* opened up a number of paths to greater life chances than had been possible under the Weimar Republic, so that the conflicts between the Weimar regime and both the *Freikorps* and the National Socialists more generally were 'thus bound up most closely with an inter-generational conflict'.[117]

What the youth groups in the 1930s and the 1960s had in common was the fact that they found their search for a meaningful life blocked by the social order held in place by the older generation. Their definition of what constituted a meaningful life was, of course, very different. However, 'the basic motivation was the same: the feeling of being trapped in a social system which made it very hard for the younger generations to find chances for a meaningful future'.[118] The differences emerge from the different kind of 'generation units' which experienced this blockage of perceived opportunity: in the 1920s and early 1930s the young people who felt frustrated by the Weimar regime were largely of middle-class background, whereas in the 1960s and 1970s there was a larger mixture of middle-class and working-class youth feeling oppressed by the apparent meaninglessness and lack of purpose in modern society. Ideologies of national identity also operated in quite different ways in the two periods, and in the 1960s it was experienced more as part of the establishment's attempts to contain the aspirations of all youth. The fact that large numbers of people had so very recently been murdered in the name of nationhood had made it virtually impossible for any young person to support any form of nationalism 'without rousing the suspicion that one was a latter-day ally of the nationalistic fathers'.[119]

Elias argued, then, that a left-wing position informed by Marxist conceptions of social and economic inequality had four functions for young Germans in the 1960s and 1970s:

> they served them as a means of purification from the curse of National Socialism; as a means of orientation through which to interpret the social character of the Nazi period as well as of contemporary society; as a vehicle for fighting against the older, established generations, against their fathers, the bourgeoisie; and as a model of an alternative society, a meaning-giving utopia against which one could critically expose one's own society's defects.[120]

He went on to suggest that part of the opposition to their parents' self-assured confidence in the superiority of European civilization, arising from the growing critical understanding of European colonialism and imperialism, was a particular ethical stance in which the younger generations 'were in many cases inclined to regard just those groups who are oppressed as better and more worthy in human terms',[121] so that demonstrable oppression automatically made any given group more or less immune from moral criticism unless it came from within.

In general terms, *The Germans* constitutes an important development in Elias's thinking, clarifying a number of aspects of his understanding of the relationship between civilization and barbarism. He pointed out that a large part of his motivation in writing *The Civilizing Process* was precisely to come to a better understanding of the brutality of the Nazi regime, since 'one cannot understand the breakdown of civilized behaviour and feeling as long as one cannot understand and explain how civilized behaviour and feeling came to be constructed and developed in European societies in the first place'.[122] In other words, Elias was advancing the very important argument that barbarism and civilization are part of the same analytical problem, namely how and under what conditions human beings satisfy their individual or group needs 'without reciprocally destroying, frustrating, demeaning or in other ways harming each other time and time again in their search for this satisfaction'.[123] The problem for Elias was both to make events such as the Holocaust – and one could add any number of other examples of 'modern barbarism' – understandable as the outcome of particular social figurations and processes of socio-historical development, and also to explain what it was about the development of modern state–societies which generated organized *critical* responses to such large-scale genocide.[124] The question he left relatively unaddressed was the explanation of the wide variety of types and degrees of responses to large-scale violence, and the significance of this oversight is one of the topics of the next section.

CRITIQUES

There are a variety of criticisms of Elias's conception of civilizing processes, and I will not be able to do justice to all of them here.[125] The ones I would like to concentrate on can be roughly grouped as follows:

- the question of continuity versus change, or has there been the degree and kind of transformation in human conduct that Elias argues for?
- the issue of contradictions and conflicts within civilizing processes, and the question of 'civilized barbarism';
- Elias's stress on the unplanned character of civilizing processes, and the possibility that intentional, deliberate action has been neglected. Should we speak of civilizing *processes* or civilizing *offensives*?
- the adequacy of Elias's understanding of psychoanalysis and the relation between psychic life and social relations;
- the validity of the link between state formation and processes of civilization, and the role of other social processes, such as the development of market economies, family forms, systems of cultural and religious beliefs.

Some points, such as the suggestion that Elias was a unilinear evolutionist, will be passed over here, when it is clear that Elias never pursued the line of thought he was being criticized for. Others are more relevant to *The Civilizing Process* and were responded to in *The Germans*, so that the question becomes the adequacy of Elias's response.

The most vigorous of Elias's critics has undoubtedly been the German ethnologist, Hans-Peter Duerr, who has written a series of books under the general title *On the Myth of the Civilizing Process*. The first volume was *Nakedness and Shame* in 1988, the second *Intimacy* in 1990, the third *Obscenity and Violence* in 1993 and the fourth *Erotic Love* in 1997.[126] To date, none have been translated into English. Duerr's overall concern is that although Elias set out to analyse the self-perception of Western Europeans' civilized nature and demonstrate the social conditions underlying 'civilization', he ended up taking on that self-perception largely as his own, and actually believed that human conduct has become considerably more civilized. Moreover, argues Duerr, what placed the ideas of Elias and his followers in close proximity to a colonial ideology was the apparent *attribution* of the technical and military dominance of Western Europe over much of the rest of the world to 'a superiority in the modelling of drive structure'.[127]

Duerr suggests that there is far more which we have in common both with our historical predecessors and with other cultures than Elias's perspective admits, and works to identify those similarities in human conduct. With respect to our relations to our bodies, for example, Duerr argued that:

> those who today laugh at a myth like that of Genesis have themselves done nothing other than mythologize history, and that this 'myth of the civilizing process' obscures the fact that, in all probability, in the last 40,000 years there have been neither wild nor primitive peoples, neither uncivilized nor natural peoples . . . and it is part of the *essence* of humans to be ashamed of their nakedness, however this nakedness may be defined historically.[128]

One central focus of Duerr's analysis, then, is to draw attention to those features of human relations in all cultural and historical contexts which produce roughly similar forms of behaviour. For example, if we agree that human sexual relations are always socially regulated and subjected to some patterned set of rules and norms, then this will universally produce some sort of division between public and private bodily domains, with the private domain constituting the focus of social regulation. For Duerr the kind of lack of restraint of sexual impulses which Elias seems to observe in the Middle Ages is simply impossible, because the patterned family relations which existed at the time required at least some set of rules governing what one could or could not do in the sexual realm, and Duerr gathers a range of historical evidence in support of this point, as well as ethnographic data to reinforce it for the cross-cultural dimensions of the argument.

Elias did maintain that he was only pointing to *relative* differences in self-restraint, that sexuality and violence was simply *less* restrained, and that there is no 'zero point' to civilizing processes, no culture or historical period where humans beings are not subjected to some form of social regulation. However, for Duerr this is a central inconsistency in Elias's work, since his portrayal of medieval social life often made it look almost totally unrestrained and free of any social regulation. Duerr draws attention to a number of passages in *The Civilizing Process* where Elias seemed to be saying, not that sexuality was less removed from public view, but not removed behind the scenes at all.[129] Despite Elias's protestations to the contrary, the way *The Civilizing Process* was written often gave the impression that the Middle Ages were understood as the *beginning* of a process of civilization, rather than seeing medieval social relations and conduct as themselves the outcome of particular processes of social change. Franz Borkeneau made a similar point in his review of the book,[130] and more recently Arnason has also suggested that the violence which dominated life in the early Middle Ages should be seen as the outcome of a specific interaction between the declining Roman Empire and the surrounding regions, 'not simply the normal condition of a society which lacks both a complex division of labour and a centralized monopoly of violence'.[131]

Much of Duerr's argument is organized around the overlap between two different types of argument in *The Civilizing Process*. On the one hand, Elias was arguing that the nature of the restraint exercised over our bodies and psychic dispositions *changed in form*, from being based on external, social agencies, to being located far more within ourselves as self-restraint. On the other hand, he also suggested that in this movement from external to self-restraint, the restraint itself became more *effective*, that individual impulses and desires became more effectively subordinated to the requirements

of ever more complex and differentiated social relations characterized by lengthened chains of social interdependency. These two
lines of argument are not necessarily the same: the first change
could take place with little corresponding change in the effectivity
of psychological restraint, and similarly the second change could
occur with little accompanying change in the way psychological
restraint is exercised. Duerr is particularly interested in the former
possibility: that although there has clearly been a historical change
in the way in which social and self-control operate, this does not
mean that the further one goes back in time, the *less* controlled and
restrained people have been.

On the contrary, Duerr argues that since 'the people in small,
easy to survey "traditional" societies were far more closely interwoven with the members of their own group than is the case with
us today', this means that 'the direct social control to which people
were subjected was more unavoidable and air-tight'.[132] Whereas
for Elias the lengthening chains of interdependence characterizing
industrializing and urbanizing societies can result only in the
demand for greater foresight and self-restraint, Duerr suggests
that 'associating with many other people also means . . . a lack of
"bindedness" and thus a relational freedom'.[133] Being bound to
a larger number of people thus means that breaches of norms
and social deviance are 'less consequential; the person concerned
does not lose *the* face, but *one* of their faces'.[134] Duerr agrees that
urbanization and the decline of feudal economic relations had
made traditional forms of social control far less effective, and that
the forms of social control which emerged from around the
Reformation and Counter-Reformation were more effective than
the older ones in some respects. However, in other senses, 'a certain
degree of porosity also arose, which was unknown to the forms of
social control in "archaic" times and which gave people opportunities for freedom which they had never had before'.[135]

Elias's own argument about the historical emergence of the
homo clausus conception of human psychology in the course of the

civilizing process can be summoned in support of Duerr here. As the distinction between the private, individual, psychological realm and the social realm intensifies, social norms can be experienced less and less as integral to one's identity, as 'external', and thus less thoroughly observed. Indeed, Elias's later comments on how the particularly German separation of the requirements of private conscience from those of social rules led to a willingness to engage in socially sanctioned barbarism reinforce the significance of this point still further. In other words, the historical emergence of more sophisticated forms of self-control alongside, or at times instead of, forms of external, social control, does not in itself guarantee an isomorphism between them, which is what Elias seems to have assumed in *The Civilizing Process*, and then recognized as false in his examination of the Nazi regime in *The Germans*. This is why Elias moved from concentrating exclusively on *the* civilizing process to include an analysis of process*es* of both civilization and *de*civilization.

Duerr is extremely sceptical about the idea that our habitus and emotional economy is linked to greater social differentiation and lengthening chains of interdependence in the way that Elias supposes. Medieval villages and members of tribal societies are, for Duerr, subjected to considerably more restraint than inhabitants of a modern industrial city. They were all 'bound up in a much more intimate way in finely meshed social webs, integrated into consanguine and affinitive kinship groups, alliance systems, age, sex, occupational and neighbourhood groups, secret and warrior societies than people in modern societies'.[136] Duerr argues that individuals were 'subjected to an essentially more effective and inexorable social control than today'.[137] This does not mean that in specific historical contexts there may not appear situations of relative behavioural freedom, but Duerr attributes this to the transition process between one type of social regulation and another, from the 'village eye' to the self-constraint of urban industrial societies. For Duerr, the intensification of self-control is less a product of any *increased* demands on individuals of more socially differentiated societies, and more the form of social regulation suited to social relations where one encounters a larger variety of 'interaction partners' from diverse social and cultural backgrounds.

A similar scepticism about the extent to which personality structure or habitus changes in the course of history was expressed by Reinhard Bendix,[138] who advanced the proposition that we should distinguish between what Oscar Lewis called the 'public' or 'social' personality characterizing a particular society or historical period, and the personality structures of the individuals making up that society or period. He only made one direct reference to Elias, with most of his attention focused on Erich Fromm, but the central arguments relate equally to Elias. Bendix argued that there was no essential congruity between prevailing social institutions and cultural forms on the one hand, and 'the psychological habitus of a people' on the other, and that people may behave in particular ways '*in spite of* as well as *because of*,' their psychological disposition', for a range of reasons including fear and apathy.[139] Bendix maintained that we must avoid the idea that people act as they desire to act, and that 'we must guard carefully against the fallacy of attributing to character structure what may be a part of the social environment'.[140] In relation to Elias, Bendix commented that he seemed to think the *same* individuals moved from being physically aggressive to being self-restrained, when Bendix felt it was more likely that people 'tried to act as they had to act, without desiring it and without being too good at it either'.[141] Rather than seeing habitus as undergoing any significant process of change, Bendix cautioned against 'the fallacy of attributing to character structure what may be part of the social environment', as well as 'the temptation of attributing to the people of another culture a psychological uniformity which we are unable to discover in our own'.[142]

In response to these criticisms, one could argue that Elias has the majority of historical social scientists on his side; if he was wrong about a development in personality structure, then so were Weber, Simmel, Horkheimer, Mannheim, Foucault, and just about every scholar who has turned their attention to the question. As David Garland summed up the issue recently, there seems to be 'a substantial body of historical evidence which would support the contention that something very like a civilizing process has indeed taken place, bringing about changes in sensibility and ultimately changes in social practice'.[143] Both Duerr and Bendix would say that this is precisely their point, that a certain orthodoxy has developed in the way we perceive European history which actually has the power of a mythology, persisting as an element of the structure of our thinking despite evidence to the contrary. It is no accident that Bendix also wrote perhaps the most thorough critique of the very notion of a distinction between tradition and modernity,[144] and although Elias improves on most analyses by posing a continuous process of development rather than distinct historical periods, the problem remains of *whether* human psychology today is so different from that of earlier historical periods.

There are two areas in Elias's own work which provide a point of linkage with Bendix and Duerr's critiques, and they may point to a way past the conflict of perspectives. First, there is the inconsistency discussed earlier about how *durable* habitus actually is in relation to social conditions, and whether a changed social context would rapidly produce a different habitus. The second is his inconsistency about the degree of *correspondence* between habitus and social relations. In most of his work he clearly assumed a functional correspondence between the requirements of a set of social conditions and the habitus developed within people from childhood onwards, but at some points he posited a theory of possible 'lag' between social conditions and habitus, with social changes often moving faster and further than psychological structure.[145]

The second area of criticism concerns Elias's neglect of the possibility of simultaneous but contradictory social processes. Until he started analysing processes of decivilization, it was fair to say that he neglected the 'dark' side of civilization, and his inclination towards elegant simplicity made it difficult to see the *dialectical* nature of civilization and the possibility of different, perhaps opposing, processes developing at different levels of any given social figuration. Breuer,[146] for example, draws attention to the 'negative side of functional differentiation', the effects of the organization of capitalist societies around the logic of the market. In remarking on the influence of Islamic culture and society on medieval Europe, Arnason also suggests that it should be seen less as a figuration of states than as 'a system of markets, monetary movements, and urban communities'.[147] Although longer chains of interdependence may demand greater foresight and calculation as Elias suggests, markets also display 'a dimension of coincidence and anarchy, which undermines the calculability of individual action'.[148] Market societies thus disintegrate and decompose social relations at the same time that they promote social integration and aggregation. Competition does not simply produce ever-larger and better integrated 'survival units', argues Breuer, it also generates 'the atomization of the social, the increasing density and negation of all ties – asocial sociability'.[149] In some senses Elias responds to this criticism in his later writings with his theory of decivilization, but for Breuer this also fails to meet his objections, because he believes that Elias still sees processes of decivilization as *distinct* from civilizing processes. Following Horkheimer and Adorno's concept of the 'dialectic of enlightenment' Breuer suggests a more dialectical conception of civilization as *itself* producing its own dark side, of civilization and decivilization as different sides of the same coin, always developing hand in hand.[150]

Third, although Elias did explicitly argue that we should analyse the interweaving of intentional action with unplanned social processes, in the substance of his analyses he laid far greater stress on the unplanned character of social change. A number of commentators, such as Haferkamp, Arnason and Chartier, argue that the result is a relative neglect of the organizing interventions of powerful social groups into the form and direction of civilizing processes. Elias's understanding of European history, suggests Arnason, 'seems to leave no place for a relatively autonomous, let alone a "pace-setting" development of world views'.[151] Haferkamp also argues that Elias did not 'give much weight to the success of intentions and plans', nor did he 'check to see when the planning of associations of action has been successful'.[152] When Chartier speaks of self-discipline and emotional management as having been 'instituted' by the state,[153] he is actually using a logic which is very different from Elias's in *The Civilizing Process*, where the emphasis is placed on the requirements of particular types of social figuration. Most social historians also paint a picture of European history where particular groups of lawyers, inquisitors, clergy, judges, entrepreneurs and so on played an active, constitutive role in shaping history, rather than merely reflecting their social context. The argument can be summarized as revolving around whether we should speak of civilizing *processes* or civilizing *offensives*.[154] Elias himself recognized the issue when he said of processes of technological change that 'there are people who bring about the technization of certain aspects of their social life, use it, and, in turn, are themselves stamped by this process,' and that 'the civilizing process is a process of *human beings* civilizing *human beings*'.[155] The difficulty is that this runs contrary to the perspective which runs through the majority of his writings.

The fourth point of criticism relates to Elias's understanding of psychoanalysis. Both Elias and most of his commentators emphasis his reliance on Freud's ideas in his theory of the civilizing process, but in fact he only made extremely selective use of those ideas, and the psychoanalytic concepts he overlooked cast considerable doubt on both his understanding of the relation between psychic and social life, and exactly how habitus has changed over time. Both Breuer and Helmut König[156] point out that Elias tended to see the superego as an agency operating exclusively in opposition to instincts, desire, impulses and emotions – what Freud called the id – and as standing solely in the service of the requirements of social relations. In Elias's own words, he saw the superego as 'the imprint of society on the inner self',[157] very much a behaviourist conception. Freud, on the other hand, saw the superego as the 'heir of the Oedipus complex' and thus:

> it is also the expression of the most powerful impulses and most important libidinal vicissitudes of the id. By setting up the ego ideal, the ego has mastered the Oedipus complex and at the same time placed itself in subjection to the id. Whereas the ego is essentially the representative of the external world, or reality, the superego stands in contrast to it as the representative of the internal world, of the id.[158]

The superego is thus anchored *within* our drive-economy, rather than simply opposed to our impulses and desires. As König puts it, 'for Freud human drives were not only the opponents of civilization, but also its basis'.[159] Emotions, aggression, and desire cannot, from a Freudian perspective simply be tamed, indeed one can only call upon desire itself in order to regulate it. This meant that Freud regarded civilization as potentially highly unstable, with control of aggression towards others based precisely in a more intensely aggressive and strict superego. Elias did acknowledge the emotional 'costs' of civilization in relation to an overly strict restraint of affects and impulses, but he believed that ultimately the benefits outweighed them and it was a problem which could be overcome. Freud, on the other hand, had a much more gloomy view in *Civilization and Its Discontents*, suggesting that civilization will always be accompanied by 'a loss of happiness through the heightening of the sense of guilt'.[160] This contrasts sharply with Elias's hopes for 'the optimal balance between his imperative drives claiming satisfaction and fulfilment and the constraints imposed upon them',[161] his notion of self-restraint becoming increasingly stable, balanced and even, and his optimism about the consequences of ever-increasing control over ourselves and our social relations.

Certainly Elias's explicit theoretical principle was that emotions and desires were themselves socially constituted, and there was no pre-social human nature which opposed or resisted the requirement of social relations. In relation to aggression, for example, he said that in the Middle Ages violence was 'inscribed in the structure of society itself',[162] and 'it is not aggression which triggers conflicts, but conflicts which trigger aggression'.[163] However, this conceptual position is constantly negated by the organization of his thinking around concepts like a 'desire' for aggression, the placement of sexuality 'behind the scenes' and, above all, the persistent use of the concept 'restraint' to describe the relation between 'spontaneous' human desires and the demands of social life. As Benjo Maso argued, 'what Elias calls a desire for aggression could with equal justification be called a pressure towards aggression'.[164] Whereas writers like Herbert Marcuse, Michel Foucault and to some extent even Freud himself, analyse the social *production* of instinctual life, Elias never put this theoretical principle to work in the body of his analyses of European social history, so that in practice we remain with a Hobbesian[165] opposition between nature and society.

A fifth area of contention is the question of the relationship between civilizing processes and state formation, and whether one can observe very similar behavioural forms in less socially differentiated cultures with no state monopoly of violence. There are a number of points where Elias put what I have called[166] the 'strong' version of his argument on the significance of state formation, suggesting that 'the peculiar stability of the apparatus of mental self-restraint which emerges as a decisive trait built into the habitus of every "civilized" human being *stands in the closest relationship* to the monopolization of physical force and the growing stability of the central organs of society'.[167]

The Dutch anthropologist H.U.E. Thoden van Velzen pointed to the problems in this perspective in his study of the Djuka or Aucaners in Surinam. The Aucaners stress the importance of civilized self-restraint, even though there is no central authority of any significance. The tribal chief has prestige but no power, the influence of Dutch colonial authorities has always been limited, and it is essentially a quite egalitarian society.[168] Nonetheless, all adults, particularly older men, 'are expected to behave with a high degree of restraint in social relationships. Aggressive or irascible behaviour is strongly censured.'[169] Like Elias's examples of European manners, there is an emphasis on relatively content-less courtesy as a social lubricant, regulation of eating habits, shame surrounding bodily functions, and so on. The Aucaners regard *Bakaa* (whites, but really all outsiders) as generally barbaric: 'rude, childish, subject to bouts of passion'. They refer to 'the Bakaa's indiscretion, but also their inability to suppress emotions and the inept way in which they conduct human relationships'.[170] In Djuka society one regulates and manages feelings and emotions in a quite stable and precise manner, and the Aucaners themselves are convinced of the sophistication of their own civilization. This is only one example, and Dennis Smith makes the same point, as does Anthony Giddens, who argued that the evidence on less socially differentiated oral cultures 'simply does not support the proposition that such cultures are universally associated with spontaneity of emotional expression'.[171]

For van Velzen the form taken by Djuka civilization can be explained in terms of its uxorilocal marriage relations: when a marriage takes place, usually the woman remains in her home village, and the man moves from his village, although he will also pay regular visits to his village of origin (in turn usually his mother's village) as well as maintaining links with his father's village. These arrangements are complicated further still by poly-gynous marriage.[172] Husbands and wives are thus engaged in a process of constant negotiation with each other and their home villages.

> In this vaguely defined situation the husband travels continu-ously back and forth, under conditions which call for the utmost tact. This situation places great demands on his powers of diplomacy. It appeals to his insight into character, his sense of social relationships and his caution. Guile, calculation and self-control are rewarded.[173]

Instead of state formation and a centralization of authority, it is the character of Djuka marriage relations which produces this complex social interdependency, which in turn generates the tight web of social expectations producing a 'civilized' Djuka personality structure. This means that a 'weaker' version of Elias's argument may be more accurate, in which there can be a variety of bases of complex social interdependency. State formation and increasing social differentiation are one possibility, but another is a particular form of marriage and family life, which appear to produce very similar civilizing effects in a variety of cultures. The strongest version of this argument would be Hans-Peter Duerr's position that every small-scale, 'face-to-face' human culture exerts powerful civilizing effects on its members. The barbarism which Elias observed in Ancient Greece, medieval Europe and under the Nazi regime in Germany may thus be very specific examples made possible by the *presence* of very particular features of those social figurations themselves, rather than indicators of a *lesser degree* of civilization.

The major conclusion we can draw from these and other criticisms is that Elias's analysis of civilizing processes is by no means a settled affair, and that there is considerable room for its further development and refinement. At various points we can say that significant reconstruction is required, even if only to make our understanding of civilization consistent with Elias's own theoretical principles. First, there seems to be a need for a more *dialectical* understanding of social relations and historical development, one which grasps the often contradictory character of social and psychic life. This applies both in relation to social relations and the conflicting consequences of state societies organized around the logic of the market, as well as in relation to psychic processes and the contradictory dynamics between our affects, desires and impulses and the requirements of social relationships. Elias himself moved in this direction in his later writings, and the issue can be seen as one of 'reading back' this conceptual shift into his earlier writings. This issue is particularly significant in coming to an adequate understanding of 'civilized barbarism', of how it is possible for dehumanizing violence to continue at both an individual and collective level at the very same time that we appear to be becoming increasingly civilized. An important question, then, is the extent to which civilization in Elias's sense actually *generates* barbaric conduct, rather than simply being its opposite.

Second, Elias's concentration on state formation and social differentiation in his earlier writings appears to require modification, to take account both of alternative aspects of social organization which can have almost identical civilizing effects, and of the diverse, often barbaric effects of state formation, indeed the brutality lying at the heart of almost every nation–state. This is particularly significant in relation to developing a less linear view of European history, to the ways in which we approach non-Western societies, and the relations between civilizations and cultures across the globe. An important area of research will thus be working through many of these arguments in relation to parts of the world other than Europe. For example, it is debatable how well Elias's analysis works even for the United States, with its weaker centralization of authority and a state with a much shakier hold of the monopoly of the means of violence. The way in which one might analyse civilizing processes outside Western Europe remains a badly under-examined area of study. Central here is the question of colonialism and imperialism, the ways in which nation–states have established a brutal and violent relationship between their own 'civilization' and the supposedly 'primitive' cultures of subjected peoples. This applies both to the ways in which Europeans dealt with their colonies, and the ways in which nation–states such as the USA, Canada and Australia based their civilization on an essentially violent and barbaric relationship with their respective indigenous peoples.

Third, the theoretical injunction to see planned, intentional action as interwoven with unplanned social processes can be explored in much greater detail in analyses of processes of civilization. Dealing with this problem will also establish much clearer linkages between Elias's work and that of social and cultural historians generally, as well as the arguments of thinkers such as Weber and Foucault.[174]

Finally, many of the criticisms appear to arise in response to Elias's persistent use of the concepts 'restraint' and 'constraint'. Elias's own theoretical position is that human habitus is socially constituted, but the notion of restraint, emanating from either outside or within an individual, implies the existence of some presocial 'nature' which requires restraining. In order to capture the social *production* of subjectivity, desire and emotions, we appear to need a different concept. The German word which Elias originally used is *Zwang*, which can also mean 'compulsion', 'coercion' or 'obligation', and these concepts probably come closer to the reality of the relations between psychic and social life. Rather than speaking of a historical transition towards increasing self-restraint, then, it would be more useful to think in terms of the relations between social and self-*compulsion*, or *discipline*, thus capturing the positive, productive aspects of the effects of social figurations on human habitus. We will return to the implications of these possible outcomes to the confrontation between Elias and his critics in the final chapter, but before that it will be useful to take a brief look at the ways in which Elias extended his process-sociological approach in relation to a number of other features of contemporary social life.

5

PROCESS SOCIOLOGY
EXTENDED

Although the core of Elias's sociology lies in his studies of civilizing processes, he extended and developed his perspective in relation to a variety of other central sociological concerns. This chapter will sketch, very briefly, only a selection of Elias's 'extensions' of his process sociology, examining the ways in which he provided a challenging understanding of the sociology of knowledge, sport and leisure, community relations and childhood. I will first examine Elias's analysis of the development of science as a product of competition and power relations between various scientific communities and groups, of scientists as social actors, and of modern science as itself part of the civilizing process. Particular attention will be paid to Elias's argument that we require a sociology of knowledge not simply relativistically to undermine the claims of social scientists to 'truth', but also to clarify their relation to their object, human social relations and processes.

Second, I will discuss Elias's studies in the sociology of sport undertaken with Eric Dunning, and how sport and leisure can be seen to illustrate the operation and effects of the civilizing process in contemporary Western societies. I will outline Elias's history of sport, from the violence of boxing in Ancient Greece to the gradual intensification of restraints in the 'sportization' of leisure, and go on to explain his argument that leisure provides an arena of social life in which 'a controlled and enjoyable decontrolling of restraints on emotions is permitted', so that sport is an example of modern emotionally managed societies, involving the production of excitement within a controlled framework, the *creation* of tension as well as its *management*.

Third, I will outline his theory of a relationship between the 'established' and 'outsiders' as structuring all social relations, and his exploration, with John Scotson, of how this relationship operates in particular community settings. Finally, I will explore a thread running through all of Elias's work, his conception of childhood and its relationship to adult experience. A central feature of his argument against the *homo clausus* view of human beings is his perception of human beings as themselves being constantly 'in process' from infancy through childhood to adulthood, old age and death, making a theory of childhood an essential element of the sociological understanding of human identity and experience. My treatment of all these topics will provide only the barest of summaries, but should indicate the basic outlines of Elias's approach to each of them.

SOCIOLOGY OF KNOWLEDGE: BETWEEN INVOLVEMENT AND DETACHMENT

One of the fields to which Elias devoted most attention, as a corollary to his concern with civilizing processes, was the sociology of knowledge. Questions of objectivity and values, the position of the social scientist in society, the relation between the natural and social sciences, these were all central to his understanding of the role that knowledge plays in the historical development of humanity. The main features of Elias's sociology of knowledge are:

1 an emphasis on the *historical development* of human knowledge;

2 an argument for seeing science as a social and collective endeavour, consisting of sets of social institutions located within a particular process of social development, rather than springing from the mind of an idealized 'subject' of scientific activity;

3 a rejection of *both* the concept of 'truth' as absolutely distinct from 'falsity' *and* a relativistic conception of knowledge, in favour of the concept of a greater or lesser 'object adequacy' in human knowledge, lying somewhere between 'involvement' and 'detachment'.

Commenting on Marx's conception of the relations between 'consciousness' and 'being', Elias mentioned two of the standard criticisms of his approach. First, like many other critics, Elias was uneasy about Marx's apparent economism, and shared Mannheim's more Weberian approach in allowing that a variety of social and group locations beyond the economic contribute to the structuring of cognition and knowledge. In Elias's words, Marx

> made no allowance for the possibility that equally structured and sociologically explicable types of oppression and exploitation may be practised, for instance, by ruling groups of a state holding the monopoly of physical power and related monopolies, sometimes even in the name of liberation from the economic type of exploitation and oppression.[1]

Second, there was the problem of whether human consciousness can be regarded as simply derivate of 'being' or lived experience, or whether consciousness also plays an active role in the development of social relations. In principle Marx himself dealt with the problem in the *Theses on Feuerbach*, but he had put the determinist argument so firmly elsewhere in his work that most commentators overlooked this more subtle version of his understanding of ideology, and Elias also felt that this apparent 'dualistic' conception of the relation between consciousness and society was an obstacle to the further development of the sociology of knowledge.

Having said that, however, Elias also felt that an important element of Marx's perspective had been overlooked by contemporary sociologists of knowledge, namely his conception of social relations as developing over time. In dispensing with the notion of 'progress', sociologists had come to neglect the whole question of historical development. Elias argued in 1971 that most sociological theories of knowledge were dominated by the attempt 'to explain the nexus of ideas, of thoughts, of knowledge, as a function of the historical situation and structure of the group within which it originates'[2] without examining the long-term development of knowledge and its links with other processes of long-term social change.[3] Any given body of knowledge, suggested Elias, 'is derived from, and is a continuation of, a long process of knowledge acquisition of the past',[4] and can only be explained as 'part of the wider development of the societies where knowledge develops and, ultimately, of that of mankind'.[5] For example, Elias distanced himself from Thomas Kuhn's distinction between 'normal science' and 'scientific revolutions'. He argued that Kuhn saw the two as too sharply discontinuous from each other, neglecting the contribution that 'normal' scientific endeavour eventually makes to paradigmatic revolutions, and presenting those scientific revolutions as too arbitrary, denying their character as progressions, extensions or improvement in human knowledge.[6]

All students of sociology are familiar with the debates concerning the possibility of objectivity, especially on whether an objective world can be said to exist independently of human observation and thought. However, Elias suggested that a fundamental problem with such debates is the underlying conception of the 'subject' of scientific endeavour as 'a lonely individual, an isolated "subject" fishing here and now for knowledge of the connections of "objects" in the vastness of an unknown world',[7] for it is this conception which generates the apparently irreconcilable opposition between absolute subjectivity and positivist objectivity. Instead, Elias argued 'that everybody stands on the shoulders of others from whom he has learned an already acquired fund of knowledge which he may extend if he can'.[8] We need, he thought, 'a paradigm appropriate to the experience that the acquisition of knowledge is a process which surpasses the life span and the capacity for discovery of a single individual'.[9] The development of knowledge is 'a process whose "subjects" are groups of people, long lines of generations of men', with a fluctuating balance between people's 'long-term interest in the connections and structures of the objects of their quest for knowledge' and their 'short-term interests, feelings and needs'.[10]

Scientific knowledge is produced by interdependent human beings in particular social settings, the unplanned dynamics of which display three features:

1 a 'long-term trend towards increasing specialization';
2 'power- and status-differentials between the various specialized disciplines'; and
3 'the tendency of scientific establishments to develop professional ideologies' which operate with greater or lesser success to enhance the status of particular disciplines.[11]

The greater the status of a particular discipline, the less inclined its members will be towards an interest in interdisciplinarity or a responsiveness to commentary from outside the discipline. Elias argued that scientific activity should be seen as taking place within powerful processes of *competition* between different scientific establishments at varying levels in a hierarchically structured social network, with the level of available economic resources dependent on a discipline's position within the network.

Sociology, in particular, is caught between two more powerful blocs which weaken its autonomy: first, within universities, physicists and philosophers, who respectively drive sociological research towards quantification and tend to undermine sociology's decentring of 'the subject'. Second, political party establishments which, through their control over the funding of social research, attempt to exercise control over the topics investigated by sociologists as well as the types of conclusions they come to.[12] The crux of his disagreement with Karl Popper was his perception that Popper was arguing for a single logic or method of scientific investigation applicable across all fields of intellectual endeavour, which Elias felt made no sense at all of the varieties of scientific establishments and their corresponding forms of inquiry. More than that, Elias regarded Popper's writings as a philosopher's attempt to impose the methods appropriate to a very particular perspective on only one discipline, classical physics, on all forms of scientific study.

He described scientific establishments as 'groups of people who collectively are able to exercise a monopolistic control over resources needed by others', and who both adminster a body of knowledge which they have inherited from a previous generation, and control the transmission of that body of knowledge, including their advances to it, to the next generation.[13] The production of scientific knowledge should thus be regarded as integrally bound up in historically specific relations of *power* within particular social settings, characterized by fluctuating power-ratios between the various groups of scientists and non-scientists. The more a scientific establishment can monopolize particular types of knowledge, the greater their power-ratio in relation to other social groups. This is why 'the striving for complete autonomy of one's own discipline and, if possible, for domination of other disciplines within the "groves of Academe" still outweighed by far the capacity for systematic co-operation', a dynamic which is 'not without influence on the construction of theories, the framing of problems and the character of the techniques used for solving them'.[14]

These observations form the basis of Elias's approach to exactly how knowledge develops over time, and his criteria for assessing what constitutes its development. He felt that the sociology of knowledge had focused too much on ideology at the expense of whatever might be counted as non-ideological 'knowledge' or 'science',[15] and was concerned to identify how the knowledge available to members of any given society is both *built upon* and *advances on* previous generations' attempts to comprehend the world around them. Rather than engaging in arguments about the 'truth' or 'falsity' of knowledge, Elias thought it was more appropriate to assess the relationship of any given idea or theory with its predecessors, with specific reference to its 'object-adequacy' or 'reality-congruence', and its 'survival value'. In his words:

> what practising scientists test if they examine the results of their enquiries, both on the empirical and the theoretical level, is not whether these results are the ultimate and final truth, but whether they are an advance in relation to the existing fund of knowledge in their field. In scientific, though not in moral matters, the concept of 'truth' is an anachronism; criteria of advance, though not yet highly conceptualized, are widely used in the practice of sciences. They form a central issue in any non-relativistic sociological study and theory of knowledge.[16]

For Elias, scientific 'advance' has two features: first, it consists of the attainment of *relative autonomy* in relation to the specific human groups engaged in the production of scientific knowledge. An exemplary case for Elias was the progressive decentring of the physical world, the development from geocentric to heliocentric, and finally to relationist conceptions of the universe. In the work of Aristotle and Ptolemy, human beings were conceived as constituting the centre of the physical universe. The work of Copernicus, Galileo and Newton, in contrast, 'shows in a paradigmatic manner the crucial changeover from the dominance of a subject-centred to that of a more object-oriented orientation'.[17] However, even this model is still subject-centred to the extent that it presumes a single frame of reference for the entire universe, whereas Einstein's theory of relativity allows for an infinite number of frames of reference, putting forward 'a model of a universe without an absolute center'.[18]

Second, Elias explained the basis of greater or lesser 'object-adequacy' in terms of an opposition between what he called 'involvement' and 'detachment', and he used the example of Edgar Allan Poe's story of two fishermen caught in a maelstrom to illustrate his argument. In the story the elder brother was so overcome by the immediacy of the situation and his direct emotional response, his 'involvement', that he was unable to formulate any course of action to avoid his fate. The younger brother, on the other hand, was able to exercise greater self-control and develop some detachment from his terror, observing how the maelstrom actually worked, in particular that cylindrical objects descended more slowly, as did smaller objects. Tying himself to a cask, he jumped out of the boat, failing to persuade his brother to do the same. The elder brother in the larger object, the boat, was dragged under, while the younger managed to stay on the water's surface until the maelstrom subsided. This does not mean that a cool head is always what a situation demands, and Elias commented that there will be times when 'force, skill, courage and a hot temper may be . . . of greater value than a high capacity for sustained self-control,' although he could not help adding 'even though a bit of reflection may still help'.[19] The point is a more complex one that particular situations will demand particular *balances* of involvement and detachment, and we can judge the adequacy of our conceptions by the effects they have – in the case of the fishermen, whether one goes under or not.

In general Elias believed that we can see a long-term development from magical or mythical ideas about the natural and human world dominated by human desires and emotions, to conceptions which achieve more detachment from our direct emotional responses and which are more 'reality-adequate'. Often Elias seemed to have a pragmatist conception of what constitutes 'reality-adequacy', suggesting that this developmental process is to a large extent determined by the role played by knowledge in power-struggles between human groups and its 'survival value'. He argued that 'one of the reasons for the long-term progress of knowledge throughout the ages . . . is the recurrence of advantages which at any given time specific societies derive in their unceasing conflicts with others from specific advances in knowledge which they make or use . . . [which] have in some case made all the difference between victory and defeat, dominance and subjection in the struggles of human groups'.[20]

Despite Elias's argument that scientific knowledge is distinguished from ideology by its degree of relative autonomy and detachment, he also believed that scientists can never achieve absolute autonomy from their social location, and there will always be a balance between involvement and detachment. Scientific thought is always located within particular social relations and bound up in specific processes of social development, which means that 'no type of knowledge can ever be in its structure and development totally autonomous in relation to the structure of the groups who use and produce it,' it can only be 'independent of it in a higher or lower degree'.[21] In the first of Elias's articles on the sociology of knowledge, he began the piece with a passage from Ernest Hemingway's *Death in the Afternoon*, where a character responds to the question, 'Are you not prejudiced?' as follows: 'Madame, rarely will you meet a more prejudiced man nor one who tells himself he keeps his mind more open. But cannot that be because one part of our mind, that which we act with, becomes prejudiced through experience, and still we keep another part completely open to observe and judge with?'[22] For Elias, all scientific endeavour is characterized by this permanent tension between the reality of 'prejudice', what many sociologists refer to as the socially constructed nature of all knowledge, and the possibility of a responsiveness to the observation and analysis of an ever-changing surrounding world, a balance between 'involvement' and 'detachment'.

SPORT AND LEISURE

In his studies of sport and leisure, Elias observed, on the one hand, that they were subject to the same types of civilizing processes as other types of activity. Although there may be superficial similarities between the Olympic Games of Ancient Greece and those played in the twentieth century, or between earlier and later varieties of 'football', Elias noted a consistent decline in the level of violence permitted and enjoyed in contests and games. Actual physical injury and even death became decreasingly acceptable in the history of all forms of contests and games; the rules governing them became gradually stricter and more efficiently enforced. One can thus speak of a process of the 'sportization' of games, especially in the late eighteenth and nineteenth centuries, in which 'game-contests involving muscular exertion attained a level of orderliness and self-discipline on the part of participants not attained before,' a process which paralleled the 'courtization' of warriors which Elias had already analysed.[23] Indeed, Elias regarded 'sportization' as an important *mechanism* of civilizing processes, allowing for a more regulated *expression* of aggressive emotions and impulses which inflicted substantially less harm and injury on the participants, a form of mock warfare in place of the real thing.

Elias was particularly struck by the development of fox hunting in England as an example of the increasingly restrained and ritualized expression of pleasure in hunting. In his words, 'with the submission of the hunting gentleman to an elaborate, self-imposed code of restraints, part of the enjoyment of hunting had become a visual enjoyment; the pleasure derived from doing had been transformed into the pleasure of seeing it done'.[24] He commented on the surprise and derision expressed by foreign contemporaries about how the English refrained from killing other animals encountered during the hunt, and mentions a French gentleman remarking that the fox 'must be worth catching when you take so much trouble'.[25]

On the other hand, he also recognized that the more or less gradual civilizing of human conduct was not a smooth process without problems or complexities. In particular, he believed that increasing civilization, the more evenly balanced regulation of emotions and impulses in response to the ever longer and more complex chains of interdependency binding human beings together, made for a potentially *dull* human existence relatively devoid of the excitement of contestation. A central problem facing societies undergoing civilizing processes, argued Elias, is how to strike 'a new balance between pleasure and restraint'.

> The progressive tightening of regulating controls over people's behaviour and the corresponding conscience-formation, the internalization of rules that regulate more elaborately all spheres of life, secured for people in their relations with each other greater security and stability, but it also entailed a loss of the pleasurable satisfactions associated with simpler and more spontaneous forms of conduct. Sport was one of the solutions to this problem.[26]

Elias regarded the involvement in games and sports of various sorts as an important manifestation of how the problem of providing 'excitement in unexciting societies' is addressed, so that what he and Dunning called 'the quest for excitement' in sport and leisure 'is complementary to the control and restraint of overt emotionality in our ordinary life. One cannot understand the one without the other.'[27]

The leisure activities which include sports and games thus have a dual relationship to increasingly civilized social relations. In addition to providing *outlets* for emotions, impulses and tensions, they also 'form an enclave for the socially approved *arousal* of moderate excitement behaviour in public'.[28] These two lines of argument in turn bear on two dimensions of sporting and leisure activities: as they are *practised* and as a *spectacle*, so that sports and games are bound up in civilizing processes in relation both to their participants and to their spectators. Some of us move between these two poles, both participating in a sporting activity at a local level and watching its professional exponents, the advantages of which include that it increases the enjoyment of spectatorship. Others are content to remain spectators and retain a stricter distinction between work and leisure.

Elias and Dunning viewed leisure activities as embodying a 'controlled decontrolling of restraints on emotions',[29] arenas which open up the possibility of both arousing emotional excitement and satisfying it, a form of organized play constituting a 'temperate emotional arousal' counteracting the stifling effects of the routinized organization of social relations in contemporary societies. This argument applies not just to sports and games, but to the whole range of leisure activities which Elias and Dunning call 'mimetic', referring to the imitation of real-life situations arousing a variety of emotions, but in 'safe' forms without the risks attached to the real thing. In mimetic activities, argue Elias and Dunning,

> pleasurable excitement can be shown with the approval of one's fellows and of one's own conscience as long as it does not overstep certain limits. One can experience hatred and the desire to kill, defeating opponents and humiliating enemies. One can share making love to the most desirable men and women, experience the anxieties of threatened defeat and the open triumph of victory. In short, one can tolerate, up to a point, the arousal of strong feelings of a great variety of types in societies which otherwise impose on people a life

of relatively even and unemotional routines and which require a high degree and great constancy of emotional controls in all human relationships.[30]

Such activities include going to films, theatre, concerts, opera, art galleries, museums, dance performances, watching game shows on television, as well as reading novels, thrillers, detective stories, and playing card games or other games of chance or skill. Elias suggested that sport 'is designed to produce as well as to contain tensions',[31] and this applies equally to the whole range of mimetic leisure activities.

Elias and Dunning's analysis of sport and leisure constitutes an important elaboration of Elias's theory of civilizing processes, by indicating the variety of complex ways in which human emotional life is organized in contemporary societies. Above all, they draw sociologists' attention to the central significance of a realm of human experience which is usually regarded as relatively trivial – the term 'sociology of leisure' still tends to provoke smirking bemusement – and the importance of the vast amount of time, effort and money invested in sport and leisure for an adequate sociological understanding of contemporary social life.

ESTABLISHED AND OUTSIDERS

Another important extension of Elias's process sociology emerged from the attention he paid to the investigation of community relations. In a study of a community south of Leicester – referred to as 'Winston Parva' – undertaken together with John Scotson in the early 1960s, Elias developed a model for social relations within and between communities which revolved around the concept of relations between 'established' and 'outsider' groups. Elias preferred the contrast between established and outsiders to Marxist conceptualizations of class relations, because it seemed to capture more comprehensively the reality of day-to-day power relations and interdependencies within communities. Elias regarded communities as particularly important types of figurations which structure many of the interdependencies between human beings, in ways which develop and change along with developments in the surrounding social structure. Of particular importance was the fact that the historical development of community relations pointed to a crucial contradiction within civilizing processes: as nation–states became more socially differentiated and more of the functions of communities were assumed by larger-scale social units, especially the state, the result was a partial disintegration within community life. Elias observed an increasing 'defunctionalization' of community life, 'until all that is left from the wide range of binding functions of communities in less differentiated societies are a community's functions for the private lives of those who form it',[32] which he saw as 'an illuminating example of the dialectic character of the development of societies'.[33]

Elias defined a community as 'a group of households situated in the same locality and linked to each other by functional interdependencies which are closer than interdependencies of the same kind with other groups of people within the wider social field to which a community belongs'.[34] His study of Winston Parva and the relations between three different communities – a middle class, a respectable working class, and a more recently arrived working-class community – suggested a theory of group relations and of the mechanics of authority and stigma which Elias felt could be applied to a variety of social contexts. The relations between the older, 'established' working-class community – the 'Village' – and the more recent 'outsider' working-class group – the 'Estate' – was of particular significance. There were no differences between them in terms of class, religion, ethnicity or education. The major distinction related to the length of time spent in Winston Parva: 'one was a group of old residents established in the neighbourhood for two or three generations and the other was a group of newcomers'.[35] The two groups displayed different degrees of social cohesion and integration, and a particular ideological construction of the relative status and worth of each group. Elias noted that there was a similarity to 'the pattern of stigmatisation used by high power groups in relation to their outsider groups all over the world . . . in spite of all the cultural differences',[36] and he argued that the dynamics of established–outsider relations had the following characteristics.

First, the status distinctions between established and outsider groups are rooted in an uneven balance of *power* between them.[37] 'Without their power,' suggested Elias about the established group, 'the claim to a higher status and a specific charisma would soon decay and sound hollow whatever the distinctiveness of their behaviour.'[38] Second, group power differentials generate a polar contrast between group charisma and group stigma and a particular 'socio-dynamics of stigmatisation'.[39] Although both groups may display a similar range of behaviour, the established group's greater social cohesion and control over flows of communication enables it to organize its public image in terms of its 'best' members, and to construct the identity of the outsiders in terms of its 'worst' members. In Winston Parva, for example, the Village organized its image of itself around a middle-class minority, while a minority of less respectable individuals and families in the Estate was perceived as representative of their basic identity.

Third, it is difficult for members of the outsider group to resist internalizing the negative characteristics attributed to it by the established. In Elias's words:

> As the established are usually more highly integrated and, in general, more powerful, they . . . can often impose on newcomers the belief that they are not only inferior in power but inferior by 'nature' to the established group. And this internalisation by the socially inferior group of the disparaging belief of the superior group as part of their own conscience and

self-image powerfully reinforces the superiority and the rule of the established group.[40]

Members of the outsider group 'emotionally experience their *power* inferiority as a sign of *human* inferiority',[41] and incorporate the stigmatizing judgements of the established group into their own personality structure.

Fourth, the shared history of the established group formed the basis of a relatively strong collective 'we' identity as the 'Village', which was a crucial element in the power relationship with the outsider group. The established group had developed 'a stock of common memories, attachments and dislikes'.[42] There was also a more cohesive network of kinship ties between both established groups, with very few kinship ties between the Estate and the Village, increasing the isolation of Estate families. These two factors underlay the Village's social cohesion and their ability to manage the form taken by gossip. Elias considered the role of gossip as a means of collective social control to be crucial in the construction and maintenance of community identity, as well as in the management of power relations between established and outsider groups. Members of the established group organized their social relations around a supportive form of gossip which Elias and Scotson referred to as 'praise gossip', reinforcing their social cohesion, and using what they called 'blame gossip' to sanction deviant members. The gossip relating to outsiders, on the other hand, was based *primarily* on 'blame gossip', encouraging the stigmatizing views of outsiders, among both the established and outsiders themselves.

The established regarded themselves as superior to a large extent because of their 'oldness', although this conception had little to do with the actual length of time a group and its predecessors had spent in the region. The housing in the 'Estate' had been built in 1930s, and began to take shape during World War II as families evacuated from London, and people continued to migrate from London after the war's end. But even twenty years later, when Elias and Scotson undertook their study,

> the older residents of the 'village' still spoke of people from the Estate as 'foreigners', saying that they 'couldn't understand a word they say'. A local newspaper reporter could still remark: 'Of course, they're Londoners, you've got to remember that, with different ways, so they are different to the older people around here.'[43]

Indeed, it is the shared identity of the established group and the perception that this group identity may be threatened by new-comers which sets the whole mechanism of established–outsider relations in motion in the first place. Elias and Scotson spoke of the 'wholesale rejection' of newcomers by the Villagers producing the social isolation of the Estate which in turn undermined its social cohesion.

Finally, an important linkage between Elias's theory of established–outsider relations and his theory of civilizing pro-cesses was the observation that the established almost invariably experience and present themselves as more 'civilized', and out-siders are constructed as more 'barbaric'. Among working-class communities the distinction generally takes the form of one between the 'respectable' or 'decent' and the 'rough'. Respect-ability was associated with 'a more articulate code of behaviour', 'a higher degree of self-restraint', ' a higher degree of orderliness, circumspection, foresight and group cohesion', all of which offer 'status- and power-rewards in compensation for the frustration of restraints and the relative loss of spontaneity'.[44] The distinction between respectability and roughness was organized around a number of perceived differences in behaviour between the Village and the Estate – referred to by Villagers as 'Rat Alley'. Estate members were seen as less restrained in their leisure time, more boisterous in their local pub and inclined to drink more than they 'should' and use 'coarse' language, more inclined to fight among themselves, less restrained in their sexual conduct, inclined to delinquency and crime, exercising little control over their children and, above all, 'dirty'. In fact, Elias and Scotson found that 'one could visit a good number of people on the Estate in their houses and find that neither the standards of cleanliness nor those of conduct were noticeably different' from those in the Village.[45] But the concentration of attention on a minority of incidents and 'rough' families on the Estate enabled the Villagers to construct a picture of the Estate as 'a kind of slum inhabited by uncouth people who lived with hordes of uncontrollable children noisily in neglected houses'.[46] A typical remark made by a Village member was that 'most of the residents on the Estate are foreigners and criminals',[47] and this type of merging of categories – criminal, black, working class, homosexual, violent, foreign, mentally ill – which in reality have little or nothing to do with each other, is a characteristic mechanism of constructing group stigma, presenting one's own established group as the bearer of human civilization itself, and the contrasting outsiders as containing all that threatens to undermine civilization.

The more general significance of the study was that Elias regarded the power relations he encountered in Winston Parva as particular examples of a model or 'empirical paradigm' of established–outsider figurations which can be found in numerous other settings and on larger scales, even if they may develop in different ways. In his words:

> What one observed in the 'village' was only a moderate small-scale example of a pattern which one can observe, often in a much more tense and virulent form, in the relation of many old established groups, nations, classes, ethnic minorities or whatever their form may be, to their outsider groups. . . . Everywhere group charisma attributed to oneself and group disgrace attributed to outsiders are complementary phenomena.[48]

He thus saw the development of an established–outsider distinction, and the dynamics of stigmatization which accompanies it, as built into the processes of group formation; the attachment of negative characteristics to an outsider group can be regarded as simply the other side of the positive self-evaluation of the members of any established group. The emergence of feelings of inferiority among the outsider group was also a useful clue to the effects of all power inequalities on those in subordinate positions.[49]

What this means is that a considerable amount of social conflict can be explained in terms of established–outsider dynamics. Elias argued that racism, for example, should not be approached in terms of the supposed differences between racial or ethnic groups, but in terms of

> the fact that one is an established group, with superior power resources, and the other is an outsider group, greatly inferior in terms of its power ratio, against which the established group can close ranks. What one calls 'race relations', in other words, are simply established–outsider relations of a particular type.[50]

Equally important was his observation that established–outsider dynamics operate, on the whole, outside the conscious control of the participants, so that in the case of Winston Parva 'the whole drama was played out by the two sides as if they were puppets on a string'.[51] However, Elias hoped that by better understanding the 'compelling forces' operating in established–outsider figurations, we might 'in time be able to devise practical measures capable of controlling them'.[52]

CHILDHOOD AND THE CIVILIZING OF PARENTS

A vital thread running through all of Elias's work is a concern to restructure the sociological conception of 'the person', the 'self' and the individual to incorporate a *temporal* dimension. His approach was to 'stretch' our understanding of habitus and the person over the whole period of any individual's biography, from the absolute dependence of a newborn infant, through the gradual acquisition of only relative independence as an adult, and then the greater dependence of old age. This was one of the central supports of his stress on the essential *interdependence* of human existence, the recognition of the *historical* character of habitus, both across generations and within any individual's lifetime. Human beings should be regarded, he argued, as 'separate people who are born as infants, have to be fed and protected for many years by their parents or other adults, who slowly grow up, who then provide for themselves in this or that social position, who may marry and have children of their own, and who finally die'. It is not only that people undergo processes of transformation, 'it would be more appropriate to say that a person is constantly in movement; he not only goes through a process, he *is* a process'.[53] Elias suggested that the 'key' to understanding what 'society' is lies in a grasp of the 'historicity of each individual, the phenomenon of growing up to adulthood', and that 'the sociality integral to a human being only becomes apparent if one is aware what relations to other people can mean for a small child'.[54]

This line of argument tends to be embedded within other concerns, making it easy to overlook, so that some commentators, including myself, have been led to complain about the lack of Elias's concern for family life.[55] However, although Elias tended to stress more that 'one cannot properly grasp the changes in the parent–child relationship without a theory of civilization',[56] closer inspection of his work reveals that it also demonstrated that processes of civilization depend on developments in childhood and adult–child relations. Childhood and family life were central to Elias's theory of civilizing processes, for three reasons. First, a crucial indicator of the existence of civilizing processes was for Elias the increasing 'distance in behaviour and whole psychical structure between children and adults' which he observed in the history of Western European societies. The development of civilizing processes involves both the continual displacement of forms of conduct from what had been regarded as acceptable for adults to the realm of 'childlike' behaviour, as well as the corresponding increasing sense of childhood as a separate sphere of life with particular characteristics and requirements which distinguish it from adulthood. 'Only now', commented Elias in 1938, 'in the age that has been called "the century of the child", is the realization that ... children cannot behave like adults slowly penetrating the family circle with appropriate educational advice and instructions.'[57]

Historians of childhood such as Philippe Ariès and Lloyd de Mause[58] were later to develop the same argument, that the proximity between the everyday lives of children and adults had gradually increased since the Middle Ages, when children shared their parents' bedrooms, were exposed to full knowledge and often experience of adult sexuality, engaged in similar forms of work and wore similar types of dress. However, 'the more complex and differentiated adult society becomes, the longer it takes, the more complex is the process of civilizatory transformation of the individual',[59] and the greater the distance between childhood and adulthood, of which the ever-increasing length of schooling is only one indicator.

Second, family life was the primary *site* of civilizing processes, the main social arena in which the development of a particular personality structure takes place. Elias spoke of parents as the 'primary agents of conditioning' through which 'the entire figuration of human beings ... exerts its pressure on the new generation'.[60] Erasmus' *De civilitate morum puerilium* (On civility in children) was a text directed at children, as was the whole concept of *civilité* and the majority of the etiquette manuals which Elias developed his arguments around. Although our personalities continue to develop in response to our changing adult relationships, it is, wrote Elias, 'the web of social relations in which the individual lives during his more impressionable phase, during childhood and youth, which imprints itself upon his unfolding personality'.[61] The entire mechanism of civilized self-restraint, the development of automatic foresight and self-observation, emerged in childhood and depended on a particular patterning of adult–child relations. Childhood is thus the main 'transmission belt' for the development of the habitus which characterizes any given society. If civilizing processes are rooted in particular patterns of social relations, among the most significant of them are relations between adults, particularly parents, and children.

Third, Elias saw the changing characters of childhood and adult experience as integrally linked with each other, developing hand in hand and exercising *reciprocal* influence on one another. While writers such as Ariès saw the 'discovery of childhood' more simply in terms of increasing social regulation of children, Elias recognized that it concerned a double-edged development, with an accompanying *democratization* of relations between adults and children and a decline in inequality between them. Alongside the ever more complex social expectations of children, Elias observed a decline in the ritualized expressions of respect for parental authority and a more general *informalization* of relations between adults and children, which he said was 'clearly symptomatic of the reduction of parental authority, of a lessening of inequality in relations between parents and children'.[62] This informalization 'goes hand in hand with a heightening of the taboos against violence in relations between parents and children, and expects, perhaps also forces, a higher degree of self-control on both sides'.[63]

The increasing recognition of the specific character of childhood and children's needs in turn demands a greater *reflexive* self-awareness and self-restraint from adults, to regulate their immediate responses to children's relatively 'uncivilized' expressions of their impulses and desires, to consider their actions far more in terms of the longer-term development of a child to an adult and to exercise a corresponding foresight. Especially in the period since World War II, there has been an increasing concern in Western societies about the role of violence, sexuality and various forms of possibly abusive behaviour in adult–child relations. The definition of what constitutes 'abuse' is becoming constantly more comprehensive and sophisticated. This concern is usually manifested in changing forms of state regulation of and intervention into family life, mediated by a variety of professional groups such as social workers, teachers, doctors and psychologists. The growing interest in 'children's rights' is only one example of this development. Just as the features of 'personhood' can only be grasped in terms of the ways in which childhood is organized, the changing character of childhood can also only be properly understood as bound up with a changing form of adulthood, particularly the experience of being a parent, which was why Elias spoke of 'the civilizing of parents'. As Elias neatly encapsulated it, the changing authority relations between parents and children today demand of parents 'a relatively very high degree of self-control, which as a model and a means of education then rebounds to impose a high degree of self-restraint on children in their turn'.[64]

CRITIQUES

Elias's theory of established–outsider relations and his emphasis on the importance of childhood and biography in understanding human experience has attracted little or no criticism, so this section will concentrate on the main critiques of his approach to sport and leisure and of his sociology of knowledge. The comments made on the former revolve around the neglect of other important features of sport and leisure, especially their political economy, their forms of organization, the role of the state, and gender. In relation to Elias's sociology of knowledge, critics have focused on the clarity of his distinction between involvement and detachment, the lack of attention paid to the question of the criteria by which object 'adequacy' or reality 'congruence' are to be judged, his apparently positivist approach to 'reality', and his neglect of the possibility of a plurality of perspectives in sociology.

A number of commentators have remarked that Elias and Dunning's analysis of sport and leisure leaves out a number of important considerations, particularly 'the interplay of economic and political forces in the construction of modern leisure ideas and practices'.[65] The argument is that the changing management of violence is only one aspect of the historical development of sport and leisure, and equally important are the political economy of sport and leisure and the role played by particular groups and organizations, such as local, regional and national government, schools, and economic enterprises. Wilson mentions the introduction of weight classes into boxing and suggests that this

> might well coincide with the rise of greater sensitivity, but the cry went up for 'greater equality of chances' in boxing because managers desired to protect their investment, because customers expected to see their money's worth, and because most gamblers wanted a sporting chance.[66]

Wilson, Alan Clarke and Ruud Stokvis all point out that the *problematic* and ever-changing nature of relations between participants, producers, and consumers/spectators requires considerably more attention than it has received in Elias and Dunning's own work, where this question is left relatively unexamined. Clarke draws attention to the question of how local support for football clubs emerged and how it is changing, and Stokvis argues more generally that:

> The basic distinguishing characteristic of modern sports is their international organization and standardization and not, as

> Elias suggests, the relatively low level of tolerated violence. . . . Even in boxing, the central problems had more to do with the organization of the sport – for example, the control of corruption – than with the control of its violence.[67]

A central dimension of the civilization of sports and leisure is thus also their increasing commodification and their place in state formation, their encapsulation in a wide variety of processes which give the 'controlled decontrolling' of emotions in contemporary societies a historically specific form.

Jennifer Hargreaves argues along similar lines, from a feminist position, that Elias and Dunning have tended to concentrate on male sports and relations among males in sport and leisure, as well as generally neglected the gendered character of all sport and leisure activities. She suggests that Elias and Dunning's 'silence about gender masks the differences between men's and women's spare time and leisure in just the same way that talking about ungendered work and leisure fails to recognize differences and inequalities between the sexes'.[68] In Elias's own work violence is not analysed as a gendered phenomenon unless it clearly concerns violence between men and women, when one of the most important features of violence in Western societies is its profoundly *masculine* character, both among active participants in sports and leisure activities and among spectators. As R.W. Connell has observed, participation in organized sport embeds 'the concern with force and skill' in the male body, which in turn supports 'the exaltation of hegemonic masculinity over other groups of men which is essential to the domination of women'.[69]

In many respects these critiques are relatively uncontentious, and constitute comments on how Elias and Dunning's preliminary analyses can best be developed into a more comprehensive sociology of sport and leisure. Dunning, for example, freely concedes that he and Elias 'have in the past been too silent on questions of gender', and that they 'needed feminists . . . to point out the unexamined masculinist assumptions in our work'.[70] Questions concerning the political economy of sport and leisure and the role of a variety of organizations can also relatively easily be addressed in addition to Elias and Dunning's analyses, making the focus broader and shifting the emphasis onto a wider range of issues, without serious damage to what have always been fairly preliminary and sketchy arguments for the sociological *significance* of sports and leisure in understanding contemporary social life. For example, Elias's suggestive remark that contemporary forms of regulated sport 'have come to serve as symbolic representations of a non-violent, non-military form of competition between states'[71] could usefully serve as the foundation of an analysis of the current relationships between national identity and the increasingly global commodification of sport, particularly in arenas such as the Olympic Games.[72]

The first criticism of Elias's sociology of knowledge concerns the clarity of his distinction between 'involvement' and 'detachment'. Chris Rojek argues that Elias never really told us exactly what constitutes either involvement or detachment, and provided 'no guidelines, no mechanisms, no drill for attaining detachment'. Sociologists wishing to practise methodological detachment, wrote Rojek, 'must whistle in the dark'.[73] The second criticism follows on from this one, relating to the question of the 'object-adequacy' or 'reality-congruence' of knowledge. Derek Layder believes that the shift from a distinction between truth and falsity to concern with whether knowledge is more or less object-adequate

> is nothing more than ambiguous word-play if no standards are laid down specifying how adequacy differs from inadequacy, and if they are laid down then one is proposing the validity of one set of criteria as against another set. Such criteria are contestable from alternative epistemological positions; there is nothing external or transcendent about notions of adequacy.[74]

At some points Elias did begin to specify some criteria of adequacy, mentioning increasing 'our' ability to control events and the world around us as well as 'survival', but these comments raise more questions than they answer: who is controlling what, to what ends, what constitutes 'survival' and how are the very different ways in which various social groups 'survive' to be related to each other?

Third, a number of critics, particularly Rojek, Layder and Dick Pels, focus on Elias's assumptions about the accessibility of 'reality' to human understanding, and accuse him of both 'sophisticated empiricism' and positivism. Rojek argues that Elias appears to 'endorse a basically rationalist view of social relations in which human interests and human knowledge are presented as slowly converging to produce a factual, precise view of the world'.[75] Pels also feels that Elias's sociology of knowledge displays a 'naive objectivist confidence about the immediate accessibility of reality and the avoidability of interest'.[76] As Pels puts it:

> Classical ingredients of the positivist creed as re-cooked by Elias include the largely taken-for-granted opposition between 'factual knowledge' and 'political-social ideals', the summary identification of the latter with preconceived fantasies and ideologies, and the resultant almost automatic tendency to identify commitment, passion, partisanship and personality with distortion, premeditation and epistemological 'pollution'. . . . Instead of 'throwing off the philosophical yoke', process sociology therefore makes only empty gestures, and bows deeply under the weight of the philosophy of yesterday.[77]

Layder argues along similar lines that Elias 'accepts one of the positivist's central criteria of validity, i.e., testability through "factual observation",'[78] without scrutinizing what constitutes 'facts' and the possibility of differing interpretations of facts.

Finally, although Elias acknowledged that different scientific disciplines do and should follow different methodologies, he tended to assume that sociology could operate within a single, unified conceptual framework, and had nothing to say about the different perspectives and traditions which have characterized sociological thought from its inception. For Elias such differences in perspective appeared primarily as obstacles to be overcome. This may indeed be the case, and there have been many attempts to develop a more unified approach to sociological theory and research. However, it is important to deal with both the fact that sociology is currently characterized by a plurality of conceptual orientations which can come to quite different interpretations of the same body of data, and those sociologists who argue explicitly in favour of such pluralism and the impossibility of a unifying epistemology.

To some extent these criticisms are deflected by Elias's own analysis of scientific establishments and his clear recognition that any 'science' consists of real human scientists embedded in particular social relations and social institutions. The fact that Elias does not spell out how we are to judge the 'adequacy' of knowledge is simply a reflection of the current state of social scientific epistemology, because there is no general agreement on that question. Pels may find Mennell's comparison of Elias's approach to Harré's and Bhaskar's neo-realism 'arbitrary and strained',[79] but this is no argument against the parallels between Elias's approach and that of realism in the philosophy of social science. Mary Hesse's observations on what has emerged from 'post-empiricism', namely:

> that data are not detachable from theory, and that their expression is permeated by theoretical categories; that the language of theoretical science is irreducibly metaphorical and unformalizable; and that the logic of science is circular interpretation, reinterpretation, and self-correction of data in terms of theory, theory in terms of data.[80]

sits quite comfortably with Elias's epistemology, and is consistent with his concern that sociological theory and research should develop hand in hand, in a permanent dialogue with each other.

Other points of criticism are pertinent but indicate how Elias's approach can be developed rather than constituting an attack on its foundations. Eric Dunning, for example, agrees with Rojek's comments on the lack of a connection between Elias's concepts of involvement and detachment and the practicalities of social research, saying that Rojek 'has correctly identified an area to which figurational sociologists need to devote a great deal more attention'.[81] The most serious element of all the critiques, requiring the most extensive modification of Elias's own ideas, concerns his attempt to present involvement and detachment as lying at opposite ends of a single axis. Elias assumed a sort of hydraulic relationship between them, with one decreasing as the other increased, but they may actually lie on different axes from each other, making it possible to be both highly detached and highly involved, for a science to be relatively 'autonomous' from its own producers and still be caught up in strong relations of involvement in its surrounding social context. The question which Elias himself left relatively unexamined, and remains to be dealt with by any sociologist making use of his ideas, is the extent to which scientific endeavour and the production of knowledge is not simply about increasing human beings' control over their natural and social environment, but also a profoundly moral, ethical and political exercise.

6

ELIAS AND CONTEMPORARY SOCIOLOGY

Beneath Elias's concern for intellectual 'detachment' there ran an undercurrent of at least two central commitments – they might be called passions, desires or visions – which motivate and give shape to his work. In developing an understanding of the position occupied by Elias's ideas in contemporary sociology, it is useful to begin with a clear outline of the main features of his intellectual 'involvement', since the responses to Elias's work are very often driven by an engagement with these more implicit dimensions of his thinking, in addition to, or sometimes instead of his explicit arguments. The first concerns the type of society Elias wanted us to work towards, the utopian element to his thinking, and the second relates to his conception of the form that human knowledge, especially sociology, should take. The chapter will then conclude with an outline of 1) the substantive sociological *questions* and *issues* which remain unresolved in Elias's own work and which will run through any continuing engagement with his ideas, along with the major areas of substantive sociological *research* where his ideas are most likely to be utilized, modified and extended, and 2) the possible reorientation of sociological *theory* which might flow from an appreciation and assimilation of his work.

CIVILIZATION AS THE IDEAL OF PERFECTABLE DISCIPLINE

Elias has often been criticized for displaying a naïve estimation of modern civilization, for neglecting the barbaric dimensions to supposedly civilized social formations. Apart from the fact that he did turn to this question in the post-war years, a major problem with this criticism is that it makes Elias out to be extraordinarily dim. Is it really plausible that someone who fought in World War I, experienced the rise of Fascism in Germany, was forced from Germany by the Nazis in 1933, and who lost his mother in Auschwitz would be unaware of the barbaric side of contemporary civilization? I think not.

More importantly, such criticism has no bearing on what Elias actually said. In the preface to *The Civilizing Process*, Elias was at pains to point out that the book arose in response to 'the experiences in whose shadow we all live, experiences of the crisis and transformation of Western civilization as it had existed hitherto, and the simple need to understand what this "civilization" really amounts to'.[1] For Elias 'civilization' was not simply an observable achievement, but more a question, a problem to be posed, about the social conditions under which whatever we might like to call 'civilization' does or does not emerge. Elias insisted on the permanently unfinished character of civilizing processes, to the point of suggesting that perhaps a period of civilization has only just begun, and we have seen that he later turned to the question of co-existing decivilizing processes. However, what this means is that while Elias cannot be seen as optimistic about the *achievements* of civilization, he certainly was optimistic about the *possibility* of its achievement. What, then, did such a civilization look like to Elias?

Generally one searches in vain for the utopian element in Elias's writings. He was far too critical of the effects of ideals and wishes in social life, preferring observation and analysis to the perils of 'involvement'. But in reality all human thought has some utopian dimension, some sense of 'the good life' which provides criteria against which to measure existing circumstances, an 'ultimate position towards life'[2] which provides the conceptual basis for criticism and analysis. Indeed, there was one point when Elias allowed himself the indulgence of commenting on what 'a very advanced form of civilization' might look like:

> One could imagine a condition of human existence where people do not need external restraint in order to refrain from the use of violence in their relationships with others . . . a society whose members are able to rely entirely on self-restraint without any extraneous restraint in observing the common rules they have worked out in the course of generations as regulators of their lives together. . . . The burden of self-restraint would . . . balance better and more evenly throughout society against the fulfilment of individual needs for personal satisfaction, meaningfulness and the wish for a pleasant life. In such a society, people who, in conflict with others – there will always be conflicts – or from a lapse of self-control under the pressure of strong affects, have broken the common rules, might . . . submit voluntarily and without the threat or use of physical force on the part of society's agents, because they could be expected to have insight enough into the workings of human societies to know that no decent and enjoyable coexistence of human beings is possible without everybody's submission to rules, and because, if any person does not keep the rules voluntarily and does not willingly submit to the penalties for breaches of the rules, no one else can be expected to do so either.[3]

Elias took up different positions on how realistic such an ideal was; here he believed that such conditions were not yet attainable and expressed doubt that they ever would be attainable, contenting himself with the observation simply that they were worth striving for. But he was usually more definite about the possibility of working towards a more balanced and less conflict-ridden human existence; indeed, his intellectual efforts would have been pointless if he was not.

Elias's vision is in many respects a dream of an almost perfect discipline, a willing *submission*, perhaps *subjection* to a humane, ethical rationality. Civilizing processes thus concern the emergence and continuing development of, to use Toby Miller's felicitous phrase, the 'well-tempered self':[4] self-regulating, manageable, calculable, autonomous citizens, reflexively conscious of the contours of the common good, willing and able constantly to moderate, constrain and normalize the free expression of their individual needs and desires in correspondence with the requirements of a considered, Enlightened civility. This ideal is what provokes a critical response in many of his readers, for most sociologists are trained to asks questions of 'rules', questions concerning the interests they serve, how diverse interests are formed, the distribution of benefit from the observance of rules, how 'benefit' is constructed. Another particularly important issue raised by such a vision is how it assesses incivility and unruliness – Elias's formulation simply raises the classic question of the relationship between civilized individual ethics and socially constructed systems of rules and norms. The Auschwitz guard who observed the requirements of civilized conduct, for example, would have stood outside the prevailing rules. Elias did sometimes ask himself whether there may be a dark side to any form of civilization, but not always, and it is this tension which gives shape to many of the debates around his work.

KNOWLEDGE, CONTROL, POWER

Elias consistently maintained that the point of sociological analysis was to improve the capacity for collective *control* over human social relations. In a clear parallel with the psychoanalytic view of the effects of bringing unconscious aspects of psychic life to consciousness, he felt that an increased awareness of the dynamics of social relationships makes it more possible and likely that we can lessen the extent to which those dynamics toss us wherever they will, enabling us to actively direct their direction and course. In 1936 he wrote in the preface to *The Civilizing Process* that one of his ambitions in writing the book was 'that, through clearer understanding, we shall one day succeed in making accessible to more conscious control these processes which today take place in and around us not very differently from natural events, and which we confront as medieval man confronted the forces of nature'.[5] He reiterated this point in *The Established and the Outsiders*,[6] and again in *What is Sociology?*, where he wrote:

The task of sociological research is *to make these blind, un-controlled processes more accessible to human understanding* by explaining them, and to enable people to orientate themselves within the interwoven social web – which, though created by their own needs and actions, is still opaque to them – and so better to control it.[7]

Throughout his life Elias was convinced that greater object-adequacy in our knowledge of social relations and processes would enable greater control over human affairs, and he regarded this knowledge/control nexus in a quite unambiguously positive light, as making it more possible to control better the barbaric dimensions of human beings' treatment of each other.

There are a number of features of Elias's position which will continue to leave many sociologists profoundly dissatisfied, but I will focus here on two of them. First, it looks uncomfortably like a 'reflection' theory of knowledge, where the job of the scientist is to reflect, as accurately as possible, an independently existing real world. In his relatively uncritical reliance on the concept 'understanding', there is little sense of the 'social construction of reality'[8] and particularly the ways in which scientific 'understandings' of particular objects of inquiry become part of those objects themselves.[9] For Elias, it was possible that particular social formations would produce specific forms of knowledge, but never the other way around: he had little sense of the *productive* effects of knowledge. For example, Elias's own observations on civilizing processes have entered the public arena and, in a variety of ways, become a part of the way many people see and experience themselves and each other, perhaps helping to 'create' the very things they are intended merely to describe and analyse.

Second, Elias's view presents both knowledge and 'control' in a relatively benign light, and there is little awareness of the position of knowledge production within *power* relations, or of the possible destructive effects of the increased 'control' for which he strove. This aspect of Elias's general perspective was modified with his later discussion of decivilizing processes, but this discussion was never extended to his approach to knowledge. The question which remains unaddressed is that of the 'dialectic of Enlightenment':[10] in what ways is improved control over any given sphere of social relations related to the production of different types of problems and deficiencies in other spheres?

RESEARCH

There are, then, a number of tensions which run through Elias's sociology which give shape to both the ways in which his ideas might be taken up in sociological theory and research, and to the ways in which we might understand the relationship of his work to that of other social scientists. The debate with Duerr, for example, revolves largely around the question of whether our habitus has really changed as much as we think it has, or whether it is largely part of the modern self-perception to want to see ourselves as radically different from our historical predecessors. Elias's conception of his own sociology was not that it was simply one perspective among many, but that it moved towards capturing the way in which all sociological theory and research should be conducted. On the one hand, many of the critiques of his work arise in response to this neglect of other sociological traditions and his refusal to spend very much time at all discussing the relationship between his approach and other perspectives. On the other hand, there continues to be a strong interest in the possibility of the unification of sociological perspectives, in syntheses of diverse sociological theories, so sociologists' attitude to this feature of Elias's work is likely to remain ambivalent.

Other issues which remain unresolved include how we should conceptualize the relatively autonomous contribution of *cultural* formation in the history of contemporary societies. Elias's emphasis on the explanatory significance of changing social relationships, on historical processes of social change, tends to undervalue the significance of forms of cultural change which may not simply arise from those larger processes of political, social and economic change. Such an approach to culture makes it difficult to grasp the contribution that particular belief systems, symbolic orders and modes of perception make to overall social change. This is related to the question of whether we should think in terms of civilizing processes or offensives, or both, and the role of the organized, deliberate shaping of history, the active and constitutive part played by organized groups of 'legislators and interpreters'[11] with civilizing and decivilizing processes. Apart from Jennifer Hargreaves' analysis of Elias and Dunning's sociology of sport, we have not yet seen a feminist reading of Elias, and an analysis of his work from a more explicitly gender-conscious perspective may draw out some hitherto neglected features of his arguments. The question of the exact relationship between civilization and barbarism, or civilizing and decivilizing processes, is still unclear, particularly in relation to whether they should be seen as mutually exclusive or as dialectically opposed sides of the same processes of social development.

There is, and will probably continue to be, debate and argument about these features of Elias's work, as well as on-going testing of his ideas in relation to particular empirical evidence. However, it will be most useful to approach such discussions and research, not in terms of settling questions of whether Elias was right or wrong, of coming to the 'correct' interpretation or position, but as a manifestation of fairly universal contradictions, ambivalences and tensions within social science more generally, which may be irresolvable without considerable shifts in central elements of all social scientific thought. The relationship between historical continuity and change, for example, is problematic in all fields of social scientific inquiry, and the Elias–Duerr debate is only one manifestation of this. The linkages between planned, intentional human action and its unplanned effects are relatively opaque for most sociologists, and the discussions of the merits and deficiencies of Elias's understanding of the issue largely reflect the uncertainty in all social science. The areas of Elias's work which are subjected to debate and criticism are thus central features of essentially contested terrain throughout social science, and our working through those debates will be most fruitful if we see them as such.

Together with these ongoing points of contestation, the basic elements of both Elias's overall theoretical approach and his empirical studies can be mobilized in relation to a wide range of topics in empirical social research, with great promise of generating powerful lines of inquiry, explanation and debate. For example, Elias's analysis of court society has significant implications for the sociology of organizations, especially organizational culture and power relations within organizations. It is also important for the analysis of consumption and the role of representation in the construction of identity. The work of Steven Shapin and Mario Biagioli[12] in the history of science, too, has indicated the importance of the development of particular types of 'civility' for the emergence of the practices of modern science. His sociology of sport and leisure can also serve as a springboard for detailed studies of the intersection between increasingly globalized and commercialized forms of sport and the formation of national and individual identities. The Olympic Games are only the most obvious example here. The position of concepts such as 'progress' and 'evolution' have never been satisfactorily resolved in theories of social change, and as sociologists continue to wrestle with their possible utility, Elias's approach to long-term processes of development and change remains a useful reference point. Civilizing processes have often operated through the prism of 'health', which serves as an organizing principle for what constitutes 'civilization', so that the sociology of health and illness could also make extensive use of Elias's concepts to analyse the long-term development of health, medical knowledge and public health.

The theory of established–outsider relations also has potential for a deeper sociological understanding of the dynamics of multiculturalism and racism, especially in the current context of increasing international migration and mixtures of cultural identities within nation–states. Elias's theory of civilizing and decivilizing processes is crucial to an understanding of citizenship and its changing meaning in the contemporary world. As social interaction becomes increasingly organized around computers and the Internet, the sociological understanding of this development will benefit enormously from seeing it as a particular social figuration based on changing patterns and lengthening chains of interdependency. Computer-mediated communication and social interaction can thus be seen as exercising a particular kind of civilizing, and decivilizing, effect, constructing a corresponding 'net habitus' among increasing numbers of people around the globe. As a set of sensitizing concepts, then, Elias's sociology has a very rich potential for the stimulation of empirical social scientific research.

THEORY

Equally significant, however, is the possible contribution that Elias can make to a reorientation of sociological theory. There is a powerful tendency among sociologists towards polarization between structure and action, micro and macro approaches, between historical sociology and ahistorical studies, between rational choice theory and sociological determinism. All the features of Elias's approach – the emphasis on social relations, long-term processes, the interweaving of planned action and unplanned development, the importance of seeing humans as interdependent, the centrality of power in social relations, and the significance of the concept 'habitus' in understanding human conduct – have considerable potential for taking socio-logical theory beyond these dichotomies, which seem to have rather outlived their usefulness. As I argued in Chapter 3, many of the supposed problems of current sociological theory can be traced back to its organization around the so-called 'Hobbesian problem of order'. However, as Zygmunt Bauman astutely observed:

> Hobbes was the victim of an optical illusion of sorts: what he mistook for the living relics of the state of nature, were the artefacts of the advanced decomposition of a tightly man-made system of social control. If anything, the worrying alien bodies infesting his life-world were pointers to the future, an avant-garde of the society to come, the few scattered examples of what was to become the 'normal state' – a society composed

of freely moving, gain-oriented individuals unbound by the now
bankrupt community supervision.[13]

There is no state of nature, and hence no 'problem of order', there
are only changing formations of habitus within ongoing processes
of civilization, of continual adjustment of human conduct and
action to particular social conditions. Although we may be critical
of many of its features, an engagement with Elias's sociology can
help us develop a theoretical space within which we can recover
those elements of sociological thought which the 'Parsonian turn'
buried beneath an opposition between 'individual' and 'society',
later to become the 'two sociologies' of action and structure,
theoretical elements for which Elias used concepts such as habitus,
figuration, social relations, unplanned processes, power and
power-ratios, interdependency, although this need not be the only
vocabulary we rely upon.

The overarching theme of Elias's sociology was, of course, the
question of human barbarism and its relation to whatever we
might wish to call civilization. Alvin Gouldner once complained
about Elias's work that violence had not been eliminated in
contemporary civilizations, it had simply been transformed from
explicit ferocity to 'passionless, impersonal callousness, in which
more persons than ever before in history are now killed or muti-
lated with the flick of a switch . . . where killing occurs without
personal rancour and the massacre of nations may be ordered
without a frown'.[14] This was, however, exactly the point Elias was
trying to address: how to understand such a development and,
more importantly, to develop a sense of what it was about the way
our social relations are ordered, and have developed in the long
term, which may make it possible to move beyond the mere
'civilization' of barbarism to its genuine elimination. His theory
of civilizing processes was above all concerned with the *problem* of
when and how civilization takes place, an analysis of the extent to
which we have come to treat each other more humanely, precisely

in order to identify how we might continue such a change into the future and live with each other with neither ferocity nor callousness. Whether Elias succeeded in this project is for the reader to judge, but as an aim for intellectual endeavour it seems hard to beat.

READING ELIAS

There are many different routes which one could take through Elias's work, with no single 'best' sequence to be followed in coming to a more detailed understanding of his ideas. What follows is merely one suggestion of a progression through his writings which would make them most approachable; you should vary it according to your interests.

For example, if you know a little about history and want to explore his historical analyses, you would read *The Court Society* and *The Civilizing Process* earlier; if you are interested in the Holocaust and 'modern barbarism' or the development of national identity, *The Germans*; the sociology of family life, 'The civilizing of parents'. If you wish to view Elias's sociological orientation in relation to him as a person, you would read *Reflections on a Life* earlier, and so on.

A useful beginning is 'The society of individuals' in *The Society of Individuals*, pp. 1–66, which Elias wrote in 1938 as an overview of *The Civilizing Process*. Next, his article 'Towards a theory of social processes' in the *British Journal of Sociology* provides a useful summary of his historical approach to sociology. After these two introductory pieces, one would be well prepared to dive into *The Civilizing Process*. This should be followed by *The Germans* to give one a sense of how Elias developed his ideas up to the 1980s, along with *The Court Society* to get a sense of their roots.

The articles 'Sociology of knowledge: new perspectives I/II' provide easy access to his sociology of knowledge arguments, and 'On the sociogenesis of sociology' is a very useful analysis of the emergence of sociology as a separate discipline. This would then form the foundation for a more informed reading of *Involvement and Detachment*. *What is Sociology?* can be examined next to deepen one's understanding of his overall approach to sociology, after which a reading of *Reflections on a Life* would provide a more personal dimension to his work. *Quest for Excitement* could then be explored for his analysis of sport and leisure, as well as *The Established and the Outsiders* for his analysis of community relations.

There are also two excellent collections of Elias's sociological writings which provide easy access to the full breadth and depth of his work. *Norbert Elias On Civilisation, Power And Knowledge*, S. Mennell and J. Goudsblom (eds), Chicago, University of Chicago Press (1997) contains a wide range of extracts from his various books and articles. *The Elias Reader*, J. Goudsblom and S. Mennell (eds), Oxford, Blackwell (1997) also gathers together a variety of key extracts, as well as almost all of Elias's previously untranslated works.

The English-language commentaries on Elias include Stephen Mennell's *Norbert Elias: An Introduction*, Oxford, Blackwell (1992), Johan Goudsblom's 'The sociology of Norbert Elias: its resonance and significance', *Theory, Culture & Society*, vol. 4 (1987), pp. 323–37; Johan Arnason's 'Figurational sociology as a counter-paradigm', *Theory, Culture & Society*, vol. 4 (1987), pp. 429–56; Artur Bogner's 'The structure of social processes: a commentary on the sociology of Norbert Elias', *Sociology*, vol. 20 (1986), pp. 387–411; Alan Sica's 'Sociogenesis versus sociogenesis:

the unique sociology of Norbert Elias', *Mid-American Review of Sociology*, vol. 9 (1984), pp. 49–78; and Zygmunt Bauman's 'The phenomenon of Norbert Elias', *Sociology*, vol. 13 (1979), pp. 117–25, although some are now rather dated. Applications of Elias's ideas can also be found in many sociologists' work, but perhaps the most consistent include Johan Goudsblom's *Sociology in the Balance*, Oxford, Blackwell (1977); Abram de Swaan's *In Care of the State*, Cambridge, Polity (1988); Eric Dunning and Chris Rojek's edited collection *Sport and Leisure in the Civilizing Process*, London, Macmillan (1992); and Johan Goudsblom, Eric Jones and Stephen Mennell's *The Course of Human History*, Armonk, NY, M.E. Sharpe (1996).

The critiques tend to be spread rather diffusely, but two of the better ones are Derek Layder's 'Social reality as figuration: a critique of Elias's conception of sociological analysis', *Sociology*, vol. 20 (1986) and Stefan Breuer's 'The denouements of civilization: Elias and modernity', *International Social Science Journal*, no. 128 (1991), pp. 401–16.

To get and stay in touch with current developments in discussions of Elias's work and how it is being used in social theory and research, the *Norbert Elias and Process Sociology* web site at http://www.usyd.edu.au/su/social/elias/elias.html provides links to the *Figurations* newsletter, forthcoming conferences, the Elias e-mail discussion group, other Elias sites and work-in-progress by scholars around the world.

Notes

1 INTRODUCTION

1 K. Taschwer, 'Wie Norbert Elias trotzdem zu einem soziologischen klassiker wurde' *Amsterdams Sociologisch Tijdschrift*, vol. 20 (1994), pp. 43–69.

2 L. Coser, 'Review of *What is Sociology?* and *Human Figurations*', *American Journal of Sociology*, vol. 86 (1980), p. 194.

3 Z. Bauman, 'The phenomenon of Norbert Elias', *Sociology*, vol. 13 (1979), p. 123.

4 C. Lasch, 'Historical sociology and the myth of maturity: Norbert Elias's "very simple formula"', *Theory & Society*, vol. 14 (1985), p. 705.

5 A. Giddens, 'Review of *The Society of Individuals*', *American Journal of Sociology*, vol. 98 (1992), p. 389.

6 M. Waters, *Modern Sociological Theory*, London, Sage (1994), pp. 196–8; G. Ritzer, *Sociological Theory Fourth Edition*, New York, McGraw-Hill (1996), pp. 511–24.

7 S. Mennell, *Norbert Elias: An Introduction*, Oxford, Blackwell (1992).

8 N. Elias, *Reflections on a Life*, Cambridge, Polity (1994) [1987], p. 75.

9 N. Elias, 'Wir sind die späten Barbaren: Der Sociologe Norbert Elias über die Zivilisationsprozeß und die Triebbewältigung', *Der Spiegel*, vol 42(21), 1988, p. 190.

10 B. Latour, *We Have Never Been Modern*, Cambridge, Mass., Harvard University Press (1993).

2 AN INTELLECTUAL SKETCH

1 N. Elias, *Reflections on a Life* (RL), Cambridge, Polity (1994) [1987], p. 86.

2 *Ibid.*, p. 88.

3 *Ibid.*, p. 12.

4 *Ibid.*, p. 92.

5 E. Cassirer, *Substance and Function and Einstein's Theory of Relativity*, translated by W.C. Swabey and M.C. Swabey, New York, Dover (1953) [1910]; *Philosophie der Symbolische Formen I. Die Sprache*, Berlin, Bruno Cassirer (1923).

6 In R. Kilminster and C. Wouters, 'From philosophy to sociology: Elias and the neo-Kantians (a response to Benjo Maso)', *Theory, Culture & Society*, vol. 12 (1995), p. 101.

7 N. Elias, *The Society of Individuals* (SI), Oxford, Blackwell (1991) [1987], p. 19.

8 N. Elias, *The Civilizing Process* (CP), Oxford, Blackwell (1994) [1939], p. 204.

9 K. Marx and F. Engels, *The German Ideology*, New York, International Publishers (1970) [1846], p. 122.

10 RL, p. 101.

11 B. Maso, 'Elias and the neo-Kantians: intellectual backgrounds of *The Civilizing Process*', *Theory, Culture & Society*, vol. 12 (1995), pp. 43–79; J. Goudsblom, 'Elias and Cassirer, sociology and philosophy' *Theory, Culture & Society*, vol. 12 (1995), pp. 121–6; R. Kilminster and C. Wouters, 'From philosophy to sociology: Elias and the neo-Kantians (a response to Benjo Maso)', *Theory, Culture & Society*, vol. 12 (1995), pp. 81–120; B. Maso, 'The differential layers of *The Civilizing Process*: a response to Goudsblom and Kilminster and Wouters', *Theory, Culture & Society*, vol. 12 (1995), p. 127–45.

12 RL, p 91.

13 *Ibid.*, p. 35.

14 *Ibid.*, p. 35.

15 'Discussion of Karl Mannheim's "Competition" paper at the Sixth Congress of German Sociologists (Zurich, 1928)', in V. Meja and N. Stehr (eds), *Knowledge and Politics*, London, Routledge (1990), p. 89.

16 *Ibid.*, p. 97.

17 *Ibid.*, p. 98.

18 *Ibid.*, p. 36.

19 *Ibid.*, p. 37.

20 M. Horkheimer, 'The present situation of social philosophy and the tasks of an Institute for Social Research' [1931], in *Between Philosophy and Social Science*, Cambridge, Mass., MIT Press (1993), p. 11.

21 M. Horkheimer, 'History and psychology' [1932], in *Between Philosophy and Social Science*, Cambridge, Mass., MIT Press (1993), p. 121.

22 M. Horkheimer, *Critical Theory*, New York, Continuum (1982), pp. 53–4.

23 I. Seglow, 'Work at a research program', in P. Gleichmann, J. Goudsblom and H. Korte (eds), *Human Figurations*, Amsterdam, Amsterdams Sociologisch Tijdschrift (1977), p. 17.

24 In J. Goudsblom, 'Responses to Norbert Elias's work in England,

Germany, the Netherlands and France', in P. Gleichmann, J. Goudsblom and H. Korte (eds), *Human Figurations*, Amsterdam, Amsterdams Sociologisch Tijdschrift (1977), p. 78.

25 S. Freud, *The Future of an Illusion* [1927], in *Standard Edition of the Complete Psychological Works of Sigmund Freud Vol. XXI*, London, Hogarth Press (1961) pp. 3–56.

26 *Ibid.*, p. 7.

27 *Ibid.*, p. 11.

28 *Ibid.*, p. 30.

29 J. Heilbron, 'Interview with Norbert Elias', Manuscript (1984), p. 11, cited in R. Kilminster, 'Norbert Elias and Karl Mannheim: closeness and distance', *Theory, Culture & Society*, vol. 10 (1993), p. 87.

30 RL, p. 40.

31 S. Freud, *The Future of an Illusion*, *op. cit.*, p. 56.

32 V. Karady, 'The pre-history of present-day French sociology 1915–1957', in C.C. Lemert (ed.) *French Sociology*, New York, Columbia University Press (1981), p. 35.

33 Personal correspondence.

34 J. Huizinga, *The Waning of the Middle Ages*, London, Arnold (1924).

35 M Ginsberg, *Sociology*, London, Thornton Butterworth (1934).

36 W.F. Ogburn, *Social Change*, New York, B.W. Huebsch (1922).

37 W.G. Sumner, *Folkways*, Boston, Ginn & Company (1906).

38 C. Judd, *The Psychology of Social Institutions*, New York, Macmillan (1926).

39 E. Parsons, *Fear and Conventionality*, New York, G. P. Putnam & Sons (1914).

40 E.S. Bogardus (ed.), *Social Problems and Social Processes: Selected Papers from The Proceedings of the American Sociological Society 1932*, Freeport, NY, Books for Libraries Press (1933).

41 CP, p. 543.

42 W. James, *Psychology*, London, Macmillan (1892), p. 143, cited in CP, p. 543.

43 W.G. Sumner, *Folkways*, Boston, Ginn & Company (1906), p. 3–4.

44 J. Goudsblom, *De Sociologie van Norbert Elias*, Amsterdam, Meulenhoff (1987), p. 45.

45 Although, a more accurate translation of the Dutch would be 'Life's ferocity' or 'vividness'.

46 J. Huizinga, *The Waning of the Middle Ages*, *op. cit.*, pp. 9–10.

47 C Judd, *The Psychology of Social Institutions*, *op. cit.*, p. 1.

48 *Ibid.*, p. 2.

49 *Ibid.*, p. 275.

50 *Ibid.*, p. 106.

51 N. Elias, *Time: An Essay*, Oxford, Blackwell (1992).

52 R. Bain, 'The concept of social process', in E.S. Bogardus (ed.), *Social Problems and Social Processes*, Freeport, NY, Books for Libraries Press (1933), p. 110.

53 R.M. MacIver, 'Causation and social process', in E.S. Bogardus (ed.), *Social Problems and Social Processes*, Freeport, NY, Books for Libraries Press (1933), p. 145.

54 *Ibid.*, p. 146.

55 M. Ginsberg, *Sociology*, London, Thornton Butterworth (1934), p. 121.

56 *Ibid.*, p. 234.

57 *Ibid.*, p. 47.

58 *Ibid.*, p. 244.

59 In J. Goudsblom, 'Responses to Norbert Elias's work in England, Germany, the Netherlands and France', *op. cit.*, p. 78.

60 N. Elias, 'Sociology of knowledge: new perspectives II', *Sociology*, vol. 5 (1971), p. 362.

61 RL, p. 132.

62 B. Nietsroj, 'Norbert Elias: a milestone in historical psycho-sociology. The making of the social person', *Journal of Historical Sociology*, vol. 2 (1989), pp. 136–60.

63 RL, p. 54.

64 *Ibid.*, p. 61.

65 R. Aron, *Memoires*, New York, Holms & Meier (1990), p. 78.

66 J. Goudsblom, 'Responses to Norbert Elias's work in England, Germany, the Netherlands and France', *op. cit.*, pp. 37–97.

67 D. Schöttker, 'Norbert Elias und Walter Benjamin. Ein unbekannter briefweschsel und sein Zusammenhang', *Merkur*, vol. 42 (1988), pp. 582–95.

68 *Ibid.*

69 RL, p. 52.

70 Fuchs had to change his name to Foulkes – the English found themselves unable to resist the temptations of coarse humour.

71 In C. Wouters, '"Ja, ja, ik was nog niet zoo'n beroerde kerel, die zoo'n vriend had" (Nescio)', in H. Israëls, M. Komen and A. de Swaan (eds), *Over Elias*, Amsterdam, Het Spinhuis (1993), p. 10.

72 RL, p. 65.

73 R. Brown, 'Norbert Elias in Leicester: some recollections', *Theory, Culture & Society*, vol. 4 (1987), p. 534.

74 M. Albrow, 'Norbert Elias (1897–1990)', *International Sociology*, vol. 5 (1990), p. 371.

75 J. Goudsblom, 'Kennismaking', in H. Israëls, M. Komen and A. de Swaan (eds), *Over Elias*, Amsterdam, Het Spinhuis (1993), p. 32.

76 *Ibid.*, p. 31.

77 SI.

78 RL, p. 66.

79 N. Mouzelis, 'On figurational sociology', *Theory, Culture & Society*, vol. 10 (1993), p. 253.

80 L. Coser, 'Review of *What is Sociology and Human Figurations*', *American Journal of Sociology*, vol. 86 (1980), pp. 192–4.

81 RL, p. 66.

82 J. Goudsblom, 'Kennismaking', in *Over Elias*, op. cit., p. 33.

83 N. Elias, 'Sociology and psychiatry', in S.H. Foulkes and G.S. Prince (eds), *Psychiatry in a Changing Society*, London, Tavistock (1969), pp. 117–44.

84 N. Elias, 'Sociology of knowledge: new perspectives', *Sociology*, vol. 5 (1971), pp. 149–68 and 355–70.

85 N. Elias, 'Theory of science and history of science: comments on a recent discussion', *Economy & Society*, vol. 1 (1972), pp. 117–33.

86 N. Elias, 'The sciences: towards a theory', in R. Whitley (ed.), *Social Processes of Scientific Development*, London, Routledge & Kegan Paul (1974), pp. 21–42.

87 M. Albrow, 'On the civilizing process', *Jewish Journal of Sociology*, vol. 11 (1969), pp. 227–36.

88 N. Wilterdink, 'Mijn slechter ik', in H. Israëls, M. Komen and A. de Swaan (eds), *Over Elias*, Amsterdam, Het Spinhuis (1993), p. 2.

89 J. Goudsblom, *Sociology in the Balance*, Oxford, Basil Blackwell (1977) [1973].

90 H.P. Duerr, *Nacktheit und Scham*, Frankfurt au Main, Suhrkamp (1988).

91 A.J. Heerma van Voss and A. van Stolk, 'Biographical interview with Norbert Elias', in N. Elias, *Reflections on a Life*, Cambridge, Polity (1994), pp. 1–80.

92 In C. Wouters, '"Ja, ja, ik was nog niet zoo'n beroerde kerel, die zoo'n vriend had" (Nescio)', *op. cit.*, p. 10.

3 TOWARDS A THEORY OF HUMAN SOCIETY

1 N. Elias, *Reflections on a Life* (RL), Cambridge, Polity (1994) [1987], p. 131.

2 N. Elias, 'Sociology and psychiatry', in S.H. Foulkes and G.S.Prince (eds), *Psychiatry in a Changing Society*, London, Tavistock (1969), p. 127.

3 N. Elias, *The Society of Individuals* (SI), Oxford, Blackwell (1991) [1987], p. 32.

4 N. Elias, 'Processes of state formation and nation building', in *Transactions of the 7th World Congress of Sociology, Varna, September 1970, vol. 3*, Sofia, International Sociological Association (1972), p. 277.

5 *Ibid.*, p. 277.

6 N. Elias, 'Sociology and psychiatry', *op. cit.*, p. 141.

7 A. Dawe, 'The two sociologies', *British Journal of Sociology*, vol. 21 (1970), pp. 207–18.

8 N. Elias and J.L. Scotson, *The Established and the Outsiders* (EO), London, Frank Cass (1965), p. 172.

9 R. Collins, 'The romanticism of agency/structure versus the analysis of micro/macro', *Current Sociology*, vol. 40 (1992), p. 77.

10 ibid, p 89.

11 C. Camic, 'The matter of habit', *American Journal of Sociology*, vol. 91 (1986), p. 1074.

12 R.W. Connell, *Which way is up? Essays on Class, Sex and Culture*, Sydney, George Allen & Unwin (1983), p. 158.

13 C. Camic, 'The matter of habit', *op. cit.*, p. 1046.

14 *Ibid.*, p. 1052.

15 M. Weber, 'Anticritical Last Word on *The Spirit of Capitalism*', *American Journal of Sociology*, vol. 83 (1978), p. 1113.

16 In W. Hennis, 'Max Weber's "Central Question"', *Economy & Society*, vol. 12 (1983), p. 146.

17 C. Camic, 'The matter of habit', *op. cit.*, p. 1077.

18 N. Elias, 'Processes of state formation and nation building', *op. cit.*, p. 278.

19 T. Parsons, *The Structure of Social Action*, New York, Free Press (1937), p. 3.

20 SI, p 64.

21 C. Lloyd, *Explanation in Social History*, Oxford, Blackwell (1986), p. 161.

22 N. Elias, 'Figuration', in B. Schäfers (ed.), *Grundbegriffe der Soziologie*,

Opladen, Leske & Budrich (1986), p. 90; cf. also C. Lloyd, *Explanation in Social History*, Oxford, Blackwell (1986), p. 162.

23 N. Elias, *What is Sociology?* (WiS), London, Hutchinson (1978) [1970], p. 76.

24 N. Elias, *The Civilizing Process* (CP), Oxford, Blackwell (1994) [1939], pp. 443–4.

25 N. Elias, 'On the sociogenesis of sociology', *Sociologisch Tijdschrift*, vol. 11 (1984), p. 43.

26 SI, p. 62.

27 *Ibid.*, p. 13.

28 CP, p. 444.

29 J.-B. Bossuet, *Discourse and Universal History*, Chicago, University of Chicago Press (1976) [1681].

30 R. Merton, 'The unanticipated consequences of purposive social action', *American Sociological Review* vol. 1 (1936), pp. 894–904; see also R. Boudon, *Theories of Social Change*, Cambridge, Polity, 1986.

31 F.A. von Hayek, 'The results of human action but not of human design', in *Studies in Philosophy, Politics and Economics*, London, Routledge & Kegan Paul (1967); *Order without Design?* London, Centre for Research in Communist Economics (1989).

32 N. Elias, 'Towards a theory of social processes: a translation', *British Journal of Sociology*, vol. 48 (1997), p. 381.

33 S. Freud, 'A difficulty in the path of psychoanalysis', *Standard Edition of the Complete Psychological Works of Sigmund Freud Vol. XIX*, London, Hogarth Press (1961) [1917], p. 145.

34 WiS, p. 58.

35 SI, p. 50.

36 CP, p. 266.

37 SI, p. 48.

38 *Ibid.*, p. 54.

39 *Ibid.*, p. 49.

40 *Ibid.*, p. 49.

41 *Ibid.*, pp. 49–50.

42 WiS, pp. 58–9.

43 N. Elias, 'Towards a theory of social processes: a translation', *op. cit.*, p. 370.

44 N. Elias, 'Technization and civilization' [1986], *Theory, Culture & Society*, vol. 12 (1995), p. 26; 'Towards a theory of social processes: a translation', *op. cit.*, p. 370.

45 N. Elias, 'Sociology and psychiatry', *op. cit.*, p. 143.

46 CP, p. 213–4.
47 WiS, p. 134.
48 CP, p. 214.
49 *Ibid.*, p. 214.
50 WiS, p. 103.
51 N. Elias, *The Court Society* (CS), New York, Pantheon (1983) [1969], p. 213.
52 *Ibid.*, p. 141.
53 WiS, p. 131.
54 N. Elias, *Involvement and Detachment* (ID), Oxford, Basil Blackwell (1987), p. 85.
55 CS, p. 208.
56 SI, p 16
57 CP, p. 214.
58 *Ibid.*, p. 214.
59 CS, p. 142.
60 *Ibid.*, p. 27.
61 D. Lockwood, 'Social integration and system integration', in G.K. Zollschan and W. Hirsch (eds), *Explorations in Social Change*, London, Routledge & Kegan Paul (1964), p. 245.
62 N. Mouzelis, 'On figurational sociology', *Theory, Culture & Society*, vol. 10 (1993), p. 252.
63 SI, p. 182.
64 *Ibid.*, p. 182.
65 CP, pp. 113, 446.
66 *Ibid.*, pp. 454–5.
67 *Ibid.*, p. 455.
68 SI, p. 36.
69 N. Elias, 'The civilizing of parents', in J. Goudsblom and S. Mennell (eds), *The Norbert Elias Reader*, Oxford, Blackwell (1997), p. 199.
70 CP, p. 249.
71 *Ibid.*, p. 156.
72 SI, p. 211.
73 N. Elias, 'Technization and civilization', *op. cit.*, p. 35; also SI, pp. 211, 214, 217.
74 E.g. P. Berger & T. Luckmann, *The Social Construction of Reality*, Harmondsworth, Penguin (1971) [1967].
75 SI, p. 19.
76 CP, p. 480.
77 SI, p. 33.
78 *Ibid.*, p. 37.

79 P. Bourdieu, *In Other Words*, Cambridge, Polity (1990), p. 192.

80 *Ibid.*, p. 192.

81 WiS, p. 75.

82 N. Elias, 'Knowledge and power: an interview by Peter Ludes', in N. Stehr and V. Meja (eds), *Society and Knowledge*, London, Transaction (1984), p. 251.

83 WiS, p. 74.

84 CS, p. 145.

85 *Ibid.*, p. 144.

86 *Ibid.*, p. 265.

87 *Ibid.*, p. 265.

88 N. Elias, 'The civilizing of parents', *op. cit.*, p. 194.

89 A. Rijnen, 'Wat zou hij er van zeggen?' in H. Israëls, M. Komen and A. de Swaan (eds), *Over Elias*, Amsterdam, Het Spinhuis (1993), pp. 92–3.

90 N. Elias, 'Sociology and psychiatry', *op. cit.*, p. 143.

91 CS, p. 143.

92 N Elias, 'Sociology and psychiatry', *op. cit.*, p. 143.

93 J. Goudsblom, *Sociology in the Balance*, Oxford, Basil Blackwell (1977) [1973], p. 149.

94 N. Elias, 'Towards a theory of social processes: a translation', *op. cit.*, p. 371.

95 K. Mannheim, *Man and Society in an Age of Reconstruction*, London, Routledge & Kegan Paul (1940), p. 16.

96 CP, p. 200.

97 ID, p. xvi.

98 N. Elias, 'Processes of state formation and nation building', *op. cit.*, pp. 274–84.

99 WiS, p. 112.

100 N. Elias, 'Soziale Prozesse', in B. Schäfers (ed.), *Grundbegriffe der Soziologie*, Opladen, Leske en Budrich (1986), p. 234.

101 WiS, p. 118.

102 *Ibid.*, p. 118.

103 CP, p. 48.

104 G. Schmied, 'Evolution und Sozialisation: Norbert Elias' Zivilisationstheorie und ihre Bedeutung für die Pädagogische Soziologie', *Archives Européenes de Sociologie*, vol. 29 (1988), p. 213.

105 CP, p. 182.

106 P. Burke, *History and Social Theory*, Cambridge, Polity (1992), p. 149.

107 N. Elias, 'Towards a theory of social processes: a translation', *op. cit.*, p. 377.

108 WiS, p. 161.
109 N. Elias, 'Towards a theory of social processes: a translation', *op. cit.*, p. 358.
110 N. Elias, '"We hebben nog niet genoeg geleerd de natuur en onzself to beheersen" Interview with Aafke Steenhuis', *De Groene Amsterdammer*, 16.5.1984, pp. 10–11.
111 N. Elias, 'Soziale Prozesse', *op. cit.*, p. 235.
112 N. Elias, 'Sociology of knowledge: new perspectives', *Sociology*, vol. 5 (1971), p. 158.
113 N. Elias, 'Problems of involvement and detachment', *British Journal of Sociology*, vol. 7 (1956), p. 234.
114 WiS, pp. 153–4.
115 C. Lloyd, 'Realism, structurism, and history', *Theory & Society*, vol. 18 (1989), pp. 468–9.
116 N. Elias, 'Problems of involvement and detachment', *op. cit.*, p. 241.
117 *Ibid.*, p. 241.
118 RL, p. 109.
119 *Ibid.*, p. 109.
120 WiS, p. 153.
121 *Ibid.*, p. 153.
122 L. Coser, 'Review of *What is Sociology* and *Human Figurations*', *American Journal of Sociology*, vol. 86 (1980), p. 193.
123 Z. Bauman, 'The phenomenon of Norbert Elias', *Sociology*, vol. 13 (1979), p. 118.
124 C.H. Cooley, *Human Nature and the Social Order*, New York, Charles Scribner's Sons (1902), p. 33.
125 L. Wirth, 'Social interaction: the problem of the individual and the group', *American Journal of Sociology*, vol. 44 (1939), pp. 965–79.
126 WiS, p. 120.
127 R. Bocock, *Durkheim and Freud*, Milton Keynes, Open University Press (1981).
128 H. Alpert, *Emile Durkheim and his Sociology*, New York, Columbia University Press (1939).
129 H. Becker. *Sociological Work*, New Brunswick, Transaction Books (1970); G.H. Mead, *Mind, Self and Society*, Chicago, University of Chicago Press (1934); H. Blumer, *Symbolic Interactionism*, Englewood Cliffs, N.J., Prentice Hall (1969); E. Goffman. *The Presentation of Self in Everyday Life*, New York, Anchor Books (1959); A. Strauss, *Negotiations*, San Francisco, Jossey-Bass (1979); R.D. Laing, 'Series and nexus in the family', *New Left Review*, vol. 15 (1962), pp. 7–14.

130 D. Layder, 'Social reality as figuration: a critique of Elias's conception of sociological analysis', *Sociology*, vol. 20 (1986), pp. 376–7; cf. also H. Haferkamp, 'From the intra-state to the inter-state civilizing process?', *Theory, Culture & Society*, vol. 4 (1987), p. 548.

131 J. Dewey and A. Bentley, *Knowing and the Known*, Boston, Beacon Press (1949), p. 108; J.A. Meacham, 'A transactional model of remembering', in N. Datan and H.W. Reese (eds), *Life-span Developmental Psychology*, New York, Academic Press (1977), p. 264.

132 A. Bentley, *The Process of Government*, Chicago, University of Chicago Press (1908), p. 178, italics added.

133 M. Granovetter, 'The strength of weak ties', *American Journal of Sociology*, vol. 78, (1973), pp. 1360–80; W.W. Powell, 'Neither market nor hierarchy: network forms of organization', in G. Thompson, J. Frances, R. Levačič and J. Mitchell (eds), *Markets, Hierarchies and Networks*, London, Sage (1991), pp. 265–76.

134 D. Knoke and J.H. Kuklinski, 'Network analysis: basic concepts', in G. Thompson, J. Frances, R. Levačič and J. Mitchell (eds), *Markets, Hierarchies and Networks*, London, Sage (1991), p. 173.

135 R. Kilminster, 'Introduction to Elias', *Theory, Culture and Society*, vol. 4 (1987), p. 215.

136 D. Pels, 'Elias and the politics of theory', *Theory, Culture & Society*, vol. 8 (1991), p. 182.

137 L. Hill, 'Anticipation of nineteenth and twentieth century social thought in the work of Adam Ferguson', *Archives Européenes du Sociologie*, vol. 37 (1996), pp. 203–28.

138 G. Ritzer, 'The current status of sociological theory: the new syntheses', in G. Ritzer (ed.), *Frontiers of Social Theory: The New Syntheses*, New York, Columbia University Press (1990), pp. 1–30.

139 C. Camic, 'The matter of habit', *op. cit.*, p. 1077.

140 D.N. Levine, 'Simmel and Parsons reconsidered', in R. Robertson and B.S. Turner (eds), *Talcott Parsons: Theorist of Modernity*, London, Sage, (1991), pp. 187–204.

141 K. Knorr-Cetina and A.V. Cicourel (eds), *Advances in Social Theory and Methodology*, London, Routledge & Kegan Paul (1981); J. Alexander, B. Giesen, R. Münch and N.J. Smelser (eds), *The Micro-Macro Link*, Berkeley, University of California Press (1987); N. Mouzelis, 'On figurational sociology', *Theory, Culture & Society*, vol. 10 (1993), pp. 239–53.

142 Z. Bauman, 'The phenomenon of Norbert Elias', *op. cit.*, p. 120.

143 D. Smith, 'Norbert Elias – established or outsider?', *Sociological Review*, vol. 32 (1984), p. 370.

144 *Ibid.*, p. 373.

145 H. Haferkamp, 'From the 'intra-state to the inter-state civilizing process?', *Theory, Culture & Society*, vol. 4 (1987), p. 556.

146 D. Layder, *Understanding Social Theory*, London, Sage (1994), p. 118.

147 N. Elias, 'An essay on sport and violence', in N. Elias and E. Dunning, *Quest for Excitement*, Oxford, Blackwell (1986), pp. 150–74.

148 P. Bourdieu and L. Wacquant, *An Invitation to Reflexive Sociology*, Chicago, University of Chicago Press (1992), p. 93.

149 N. Elias, 'Soziale Prozesse', *op. cit.*, p. 237.

150 N. Elias, 'The civilizing of parents', *op. cit.*, p. 191.

151 P. Bourdieu and L. Wacquant, *An Invitation to Reflexive Sociology*, *op. cit.*, p. 51, emphasis added.

152 *Ibid.*, p. 51.

153 D. Pels, 'Elias and the politics of theory', *op. cit.*, p. 181.

154 *Ibid.*, p. 181.

4 ON CIVILIZING PROCESSES

1 N. Elias, *The Court Society* (CS), New York, Pantheon (1983) [1969], p. 40.

2 *Ibid.*, p. 36.

3 *Ibid.*, p. 38.

4 *Ibid.*, p. 40.

5 *Ibid.*, p. 92.

6 *Ibid.*, p. 92.

7 *Ibid.*, p. 111.

8 *Ibid.*, p. 111.

9 *Ibid.*, p. 115.

10 *Ibid.*, p. 112.

11 *Ibid.*, p. 113.

12 *Ibid.*, p. 104.

13 *Ibid.*, p. 105, emphasis added.

14 *Ibid.*, p. 104.

15 *Ibid.*, p. 105.

16 *Ibid.*, p. 206.

17 *Ibid.*, p. 206.

18 *Ibid.*, p. 207.

19 *Ibid.*, p. 168.

20 *Ibid.*, p. 3.

21 *Ibid.*, p. 76.

22 *Ibid.*, p. 158.

23 *Ibid.*, p. 140.

24 N. Elias, *The Civilizing Process* (CP), Oxford, Blackwell (1994) [1939], p. 41.

25 *Ibid.*, p. 41.

26 In D. Schöttker, 'Norbert Elias und Walter Benjamin. Ein unbekannter briefwechsel und sein Zusammenhang', *Merkur*, vol. 42, no. 7 (1988), p. 94.

27 *Ibid.*

28 CP, p. 249.

29 *Ibid.*, p. 49.

30 *Ibid.*, p. 48.

31 *Ibid.*, p. 44.

32 J Huizinga, *The Waning of the Middle Ages*, London, Arnold (1924).

33 CP, p. 50.

34 *Ibid.*, p. 87.

35 *Ibid.*, p. 99.

36 *Ibid.*, pp. 120–1, Elias's italics.

37 *Ibid.*, p. 47.

38 *Ibid.*, p. 76.

39 *Ibid.*, p. 159.

40 N. Elias, 'The Civilizing Process revisited: interview with Stanislas Fontaine', *Theory & Society*, vol. 5 (1978), p. 248.

41 CP, p. 159.

42 *Ibid.*, p. 159.

43 *Ibid.*, p. 88.

44 *Ibid.*, p. 64.

45 *Ibid.*, p. 63.

46 *Ibid.*, p. 95.

47 *Ibid.*, p. 113.

48 *Ibid.*, p. 154.

49 *Ibid.*, p. 153.

50 *Ibid.*, p. 153.

51 *Ibid.*, p. 153.

52 *Ibid.*, p. 154.

53 *Ibid.*, p. 288.

54 *Ibid.*, p. 269.

55 *Ibid.*, p. 457.

56 *Ibid.*, p. 342.

57 *Ibid.*, p. 347.

58 *Ibid.*, p. 347.

59 *Ibid.*, p. 397.

60 *Ibid.*, p. 397.

61 *Ibid.*, p. 348.

62 *Ibid.*, p. 476.

63 *Ibid.*, p. 447; translation modified.

64 *Ibid.*, p. 450.

65 *Ibid.*, p. 448.

66 *Ibid.*, p. 452.

67 *Ibid.*, p. 445.

68 *Ibid.*, p. 445.

69 *Ibid.*, p. 456.

70 *Ibid.*, p. 395.

71 *Ibid.*, p. 452.

72 *Ibid.*, p. 453.

73 *Ibid.*, pp. 445–6.

74 N. Elias, *Time: an essay*, Oxford, Blackwell (1992), p. 34.

75 See also E.P. Thompson, 'Time, work discipline and industrial capitalism', *Past & Present*, vol. 38 (1967), pp. 56–97.

76 CP, p. 458.

77 *Ibid.*, p. 458.

78 *Ibid.*, p. 131.

79 *Ibid.*, p. 48.

80 *Ibid.*, p. 524.

81 N. Elias, *The Germans* (TG), Cambridge: Polity (1996), p. 173.

82 CP, p. 274.

83 I Wallerstein, *The Politics of the World Economy*, Cambridge, Cambridge University Press (1984); 'World-systems analysis', in A. Giddens and J. Turner (eds), *Social Theory Today*, Cambridge, Polity (1987), pp. 309–24; R. Robertson, *Globalization*, London, Sage (1992).

84 CP, p. 542.

85 J. Arnason, 'Civilization, culture and power: reflections on Norbert Elias' genealogy of the West', *Thesis Eleven*, no. 24 (1989), p. 65.

86 H. Haferkamp, 'From the intra-state to the inter-state civilizing process?', *Theory, Culture & Society*, vol. 4 (1987), p. 546.

87 TG, p. 1.

88 *Ibid.*, p. 7.

89 *Ibid.*, p. 15.

90 *Ibid.*, p. 19.

91 CP, p. 253.

92 TG, p. 196; also p. 317.

93 *Ibid.*, p. 162.

94 *Ibid.*, p. 161.

95 *Ibid.*, p. 334.

96 *Ibid.*, p. 151

97 *Ibid.*, p. 352.

98 *Ibid.*, p. 329.

99 *Ibid.*, p. 338.

100 *Ibid.*, p. 338.

101 *Ibid.*, p. 341.

102 *Ibid.*, p. 383.

103 *Ibid.*, p. 175.

104 C. Wouters, 'Informalization and the civilising process', in P. Gleichman, J. Goudsblom and H. Korte (eds), *Human Figurations*, Amsterdam, Amsterdams Sociologisch Tijdschrift (1977), p. 448.

105 N. Elias, 'Soziale Prozesse', in B. Schäfers (ed.), *Grundbegriffe der Soziologie*, Opladen, Leske en Budrich (1986), p. 235.

106 TG, p. 308.

107 S. Breuer, 'The denouements of civilization: Elias and modernity', *International Social Science Journal*, no. 128 (1991), pp. 405–6.

108 CP, p. 115.

109 C. Wouters, 'Informalization and the civilising process', *op. cit.*

110 TG, p. 37.

111 *Ibid.*, p. 25.

112 M. Foucault, 'Governmentality', *Ideology & Consciousness*, vol. 6 (1979), pp. 5–21; G. Burchell, C. Gordon and P. Miller (eds), *The Foucault Effect*, London, Harvester Wheatsheaf (1991).

113 K. Mannheim, 'The problem of generations' [1928], *Essays on the Sociology of Knowledge*, New York, Oxford University Press (1952), pp. 276–322.

114 TG, p. 242.

115 *Ibid.*, pp. 243–4.

116 *Ibid.*, p. 243.

117 *Ibid.*, p. 247.

118 *Ibid.*, p. 198

119 *Ibid.*, p. 261.

120 *Ibid.*, pp. 253–4.

121 *Ibid.*, p. 261.

122 *Ibid.*, pp. 444–5.

123 *Ibid.*, p. 31.

124 *Ibid.*, p. 445.

125 See also S. Mennell, *Norbert Elias; An Introduction*, Oxford, Blackwell (1992): 227–50; R. van Krieken, 'Violence, self-discipline and modernity: beyond the "civilizing process"', *Sociological Review*, vol. 37 (1989), pp. 193–218.

126 H.P. Duerr, *Nacktheit und Scham*, Frankfurt am Main, Suhrkamp (1988); *Intimität*, Frankfurt am Main, Suhrkamp (1990); *Obszönität und Gewalt*, Frankfurt am Main, Suhrkamp (1993); *Der erotische leib*, Frankfurt am Main, Suhrkamp (1997).

127 H.P. Duerr, *Obszönität und Gewalt*, *op. cit.*, p. 12.

128 H.P. Duerr, *Nacktheit und Scham*, *op. cit.*, p. 12.

129 H.P. Duerr, *Intimität*, *op. cit.*, p. 12.

130 F. Borkeneau, 'Review of Elias I', *Sociological Review*, vol. 30 (1938), pp. 308–11.

131 J. Arnason, 'Civilization, culture and power: reflections on Norbert Elias' genealogy of the West', *op. cit.*, pp. 54–5.

132 H.P. Duerr, *Nacktheit und Scham*, *op. cit.*, p. 10.

133 *Ibid.*, p. 11.

134 H.P. Duerr, *Obszönität und Gewalt*, *op. cit.*, p. 28.

135 H.P. Duerr, *Intimität*, *op. cit.*, p. 24.

136 H.P. Duerr, *Obszönität und Gewalt*, *op. cit.*, pp. 26–7.

137 *Ibid.*, p. 26.

138 R. Bendix, 'Compliant behaviour and individual personality', *American Journal of Sociology*, vol. 58 (1952), pp. 292–303.

139 *Ibid.*, p. 297.

140 *Ibid.*, 301.

141 *Ibid.*, 302.

142 *Ibid.*, 301.

143 D. Garland, *Punishment and Modern Society*, Chicago, University of Chicago Press (1990), p. 233.

144 R. Bendix, 'Tradition and modernity reconsidered', *Comparative Studies in Society & History*, vol. 9 (1967), pp. 292–346.

145 TG, p. 337; N. Elias, 'Technization and civilization' [1986], *Theory, Culture & Society*, vol. 12 (1995), pp. 30, 35.

146 S. Breuer, 'The denouements of civilization: Elias and modernity', *op. cit.*, pp. 401–16.

147 J. Arnason, 'Civilization, culture and power: reflections on Norbert Elias' genealogy of the West', *op. cit.*, p. 55.

148 S. Breuer, 'The denouements of civilization: Elias and modernity', *op. cit.*, p. 405.

149 *Ibid.*, p. 407.

150 *Ibid.*, p. 414.

151 J. Arnason, 'Civilization, culture and power: reflections on Norbert Elias' genealogy of the West', *op. cit.*, p. 56.

152 H. Haferkamp, 'From the intra-state to the inter-state civilizing process?', *op. cit.*, p, 556.

153 R. Chartier, 'Introduction', in R. Chartier (ed.), *A History of Private Life, Vol. III: Passions of the Renaissance*, Cambridge, Mass., Harvard University Press (1989), p. 16.

154 R. van Krieken, 'The organisation of the soul: Elias and Foucault on discipline and the self', *Archives Européennes de Sociologie*, vol. 31 (1990), pp. 353–71.

155 N. Elias, 'Technization and civilization', *op. cit.* (1995), p. 19.

156 H König, 'Norbert Elias und Sigmund Freud: Der Prozeß der Zivilisation', *Leviathan* vol. 21 (1993), pp. 205–21.

157 CP, p. 105.

158 S. Freud, 'The Ego and the Id' [1923], *Standard Edition of the Complete Psychological Works of Sigmund Freud Vol. XIX*, London, Hogarth Press (1961), p. 36.

159 H König, 'Norbert Elias und Sigmund Freud: Der Prozeß der Zivilisation', *op. cit.*, p. 207; S. Breuer, 'The denouements of civilisation', *op. cit.*, p. 408.

160 S. Freud, *Civilization and its Discontents* [1930], *Standard Edition of the Complete Psychological Works of Sigmund Freud Vol. XXI*, London, Hogarth Press (1961), p. 134.

161 CP, p. 524.

162 N. Elias, 'The civilizing process revisited: interview with Stanislas Fontaine', *op. cit.*, p. 248; also CP, p. 159.

163 TG, p. 461.

164 B. Maso, 'Ontwikkelingen van de aanvalslust in de late middeleeuwen', *Sociologische Gids*, vol. 29 (1982), p. 322.

165 T. Hobbes, *De Cive*, Oxford, Clarendon Press (1983), p. 72.

166 R. van Krieken, 'Violence, self-discipline and modernity beyond the "civilizing process"', *op. cit.*

167 CP, p. 447, emphasis added, translation modified.

168 H.U.E. van Velzen, 'De Aukaanse (Djoeka) Beschaving' *Sociologische Gids*, vol. 29 (1982), pp. 243–78.

169 H.U.E. van Velzen, 'The Djuka civilization', *Netherlands Journal of Sociology*, vol. 20 (1984), p. 88.

170 H.U.E. van Velzen, 'De Aukaanse (Djoeka) Beschaving', *op. cit.*, p. 247.

171 D. Smith, 'Norbert Elias – established or outsider?', *Sociological Review*, vol. 32 (1984), pp. 367–89; A. Giddens, *The Constitution of Society*, Cambridge, Polity (1984), p. 242.

172 H.U.E. van Velzen, 'The Djuka civilization', *op. cit.*, p. 90.

173 *Ibid.*, p. 91.

174 R van Krieken, 'The organisation of the soul: Elias and Foucault on discipline and the self', *op. cit.*, pp. 353–71; 'Social discipline and state formation: Weber and Oestreich on the historical sociology of subjectivity', *Amsterdams Sociologisch Tijdschrift*, vol. 17 (1989), pp. 3–28.

5 PROCESS SOCIOLOGY EXTENDED

1 N. Elias, 'Sociology of knowledge: new perspectives', *Sociology* vol. 5 (1971), p. 155.

2 *Ibid.*, p. 158.

3 *Ibid.*, p. 161.

4 *Ibid.*, p. 158.

5 *Ibid.*, p. 159.

6 *Ibid.*, p. 168.

7 *Ibid.*, p. 165.

8 *Ibid.*, p. 165.

9 *Ibid.*, p. 165.

10 *Ibid.*, pp. 165–6.

11 N. Elias, 'Scientific establishments', in N. Elias, R. Whitley and H.G. Martins (eds), *Scientific Establishments and Hierarchies*, Dordrecht, Reidel (1982), p. 26.

12 *Ibid.*, pp. 54–6.

13 *Ibid.*, p. 40.

14 *Ibid.*, pp. 44–5.

15 N. Elias, 'Sociology of knowledge: new perspectives', *op. cit.*, pp. 161–2.

16 *Ibid.*, p. 358.

17 *Ibid.*, p. 359.

18 *Ibid.*, p. 360.

19 N. Elias, *Involvement and Detachment* (ID), Oxford, Blackwell (1987), p. 47.

20 N. Elias, 'Sociology of knowledge: new perspectives', *op. cit.*, p. 160.

21 *Ibid.*, p. 365.

22 N. Elias, 'Problems of involvement and detachment', *British Journal of Sociology*, vol. 7 (1956), p. 226.

23 N. Elias, 'An essay on sport and violence', in N. Elias and E. Dunning, *Quest for Excitement: Sport and Leisure in the Civilizing Process*, Oxford, Blackwell (1986), p. 151.

24 *Ibid.*, p. 162.

25 *Ibid.*, p. 160.

26 *Ibid.*, p. 165.

27 N. Elias, 'The quest for excitement in leisure', in N. Elias and E. Dunning, *Quest for Excitement*, Oxford, Blackwell (1986), p. 66.

28 *Ibid.*, p. 65, emphasis added.

29 N. Elias, 'Leisure in the spare-time spectrum', in N. Elias and E. Dunning, *Quest for Excitement*, Oxford, Blackwell (1986), p. 96.

30 *Ibid.*, p. 125.

31 N. Elias, 'An essay on sport and violence', *op. cit.*, p. 159.

32 N. Elias, 'Towards a theory of communities', in C. Bell and H. Newby (eds), *The Sociology of Community*, London, Frank Cass (1974), p. xxix.

33 *Ibid.*, p. xxxiii.

34 *Ibid.*, p. xix.

35 N. Elias and J.L. Scotson, *The Established and the Outsiders*, London, Frank Cass (1965), pp. xxi–xxii.

36 *Ibid.*, p. xxvi.

37 *Ibid.*, p. xx.

38 *Ibid.*, p. 155.

39 *Ibid.*, p. xix.

40 *Ibid.*, pp. 158–9.

41 *Ibid.*, p. xxvi.

42 *Ibid.*, p. xxxviii.

43 *Ibid.*, p. 19.

44 *Ibid.*, p. 153.

45 *Ibid.*, p. 81.

46 *Ibid.*, p. 81.

47 *Ibid.*, p. 88.

48 *Ibid.*, p. 104.

49 *Ibid.*, p. xxvi.

50 *Ibid.*, p. xxx.

51 *Ibid.*, p. lii.

52 *Ibid.*, p. 173.

53 N. Elias, *What is Sociology?* London, Hutchinson (1978) [1970], p. 118.

54 N. Elias, *The Society of Individuals* (SI), Oxford, Basil Blackwell (1991), pp. 25–6.

55 G. Mosse, 'Review of *The Civilizing Process: The History of Manners*',

New German Critique, vol. 15 (1978), pp. 178–83; R. van Krieken, 'Violence, self-discipline and modernity: beyond the "civilizing process"', *Sociological Review*, vol. 37 (1989), pp. 193–218.

56 N. Elias, 'The civilizing of parents', in J. Goudsblom and S. Mennell (eds), *The Norbert Elias Reader*, Oxford, Blackwell (1997), p. 201.

57 N. Elias, *The Civilizing Process* (CP), Oxford, Blackwell (1994) [1939], p. 138.

58 P. Ariés, *Centuries of Childhood*, London, Jonathan Cape (1962) and L. de Mause, *The Evolution of Childhood*, New York, Harper & Row (1974).

59 N. Elias, 'The civilizing of parents', *op. cit.*, p. 202.

60 CP, p. 115.

61 *Ibid.*, p. 454.

62 N. Elias, 'The civilizing of parents', *op. cit.*, p. 207.

63 *Ibid.*, p. 207.

64 *Ibid.*, p. 208.

65 J. Wilson, 'Cleaning up the game: perspectives on the evolution of professional sports', in E. Dunning and C. Rojek (eds), *Sport and Leisure in the Civilizing Process*, London, Macmillan (1992), p. 79.

66 *Ibid.*, p. 80.

67 R. Stokvis, 'Sport and civilization: is violence the central problem?', in E. Dunning and C. Rojek (eds), *Sport and Leisure in the Civilizing Process*, London, Macmillan (1992), p. 134.

68 J. Hargreaves, 'Sex, gender and the body in sport and leisure: has there been a civilizing process?', in E. Dunning and C. Rojek (eds), *Sport and Leisure in the Civilizing Process*, London, Macmillan (1992), p. 164.

69 R.W. Connell, *Gender and Power*, Sydney, Allen & Unwin (1987), pp. 177–8.

70 E. Dunning, 'Figurational sociology and the sociology of sport: some concluding remarks', in E. Dunning and C. Rojek (eds), *Sport and Leisure in the Civilizing Process*, London, Macmillan (1992), p. 255.

71 N. Elias, 'Introduction', in N. Elias and E. Dunning, *Quest for Excitement*, Oxford, Blackwell (1986), p. 23.

72 J. Maguire, 'Towards a sociological theory of sport and the emotions: a process-sociological perspective', in E. Dunning and C. Rojek (eds), *Sport and Leisure in the Civilizing Process*, London, Macmillan (1992), pp. 96–120.

73 C. Rojek, 'Problems of involvement and detachment in the writings of Norbert Elias', *British Journal of Sociology*, vol. 37 (1986), p. 591.

74 D. Layder, 'Social reality as figuration: a critique of Elias's conception of sociological analysis', *Sociology*, vol. 20 (1986), p. 383.

75 C. Rojek, 'Problems of involvement and detachment in the writings of Norbert Elias', *op. cit.*, p. 592.

76 D. Pels, 'Elias and the politics of theory', *Theory, Culture & Society*, vol. 8 (1991), p. 181.

77 *Ibid.*, p. 181.

78 D. Layder, 'Social reality as figuration: a critique of Elias's conception of sociological analysis', *op. cit.*, p. 382.

79 D. Pels, 'Elias and the politics of theory', *op. cit.*, p. 181.

80 M. Hesse, *Revolutions and Reconstruction in the Philosophy of Science*, Brighton, Harvester (1980), p. 173.

81 E. Dunning, 'Figurational sociology and the sociology of sport: some concluding remarks', in E. Dunning and C. Rojek (eds), *Sport and Leisure in the Civilizing Process*, London, Macmillan (1992), p. 254.

6 ELIAS AND CONTEMPORARY SOCIOLOGY

1 N. Elias, *The Civilizing Process* (CP), Oxford, Blackwell (1994) [1939], p. xvi.

2 M. Weber, 'Science as a vocation' [1918], in H.H. Gerth and C.W. Mills (eds), *From Max Weber*, London, Routledge & Kegan Paul (1948), p. 143.

3 N. Elias, *Involvement and Detachment*, Oxford, Blackwell (1987), p. 76.

4 T. Miller, *The Well-Tempered Self*, Baltimore, Johns Hopkins Press (1993).

5 CP, p xvi.

6 N. Elias and J.L. Scotson, *The Established and the Outsiders*, London, Frank Cass (1965), pp. 172–3.

7 N. Elias, *What is Sociology?* London, Hutchinson (1978), pp.153–4.

8 P. Berger and T. Luckmann, *The Social Construction of Reality*, Harmondsworth, Penguin (1971) [1967].

9 G. Devereux, *From Anxiety to Method in the Behavioral Sciences*, The Hague, Mouton (1968).

10 T. Adorno and M. Horkheimer, *The Dialectic of Enlightenment*, New York, Herder & Herder (1972).

11 Z. Bauman, *Legislators and Interpreters*, Cambridge, Polity (1987).

12 S. Shapin, *A Social History of Truth*, Chicago, University of Chicago Press (1994); M. Biagioli, *Galileo, Courtier*, Chicago, University of Chicago Press (1993).

13 Z. Bauman, *Legislators and Interpreters*, Cambridge, Polity (1987), p. 54.
14 A. Gouldner, 'Doubts about the uselessness of men and the meaning of the civilizing process', *Theory & Society*, vol. 10 (1981), p. 418.

BIBLIOGRAPHY

This bibliography lists those of Elias's books, articles and interviews which have been published in English. More complete bibliographies can be found in S. Mennell, *Norbert Elias: An Introduction*, Oxford, Blackwell (1992) and in H. Kuzmics and I. Morth (eds), *Der unendliche Prozeß der Zivilisation*, Frankfurt, Campus (1991). Where it concerns a translation, the date of original publication is provided [in square brackets].

1950 'Studies in the genesis of the naval profession', *British Journal of Sociology*, vol. 1, no. 4, pp. 291–309.

1956 'Problems of involvement and detachment', *British Journal of Sociology*, vol. 7, no. 3, pp. 226–52.

1965 *The Established and the Outsiders* [with John L. Scotson], London, Frank Cass.

1966 'Dynamics of sports groups with special reference to football' [with Eric Dunning], *British Journal of Sociology*, vol. 17, no. 4, pp. 388–402.

1969 'Sociology and psychiatry', in S.H. Foulkes and G. Stewart Prince (eds), *Psychiatry in a Changing Society*, London, Tavistock, pp. 117–44.
'The quest for excitement in leisure' [with Eric Dunning], *Sport & Leisure*, vol. 2, pp. 50–85.

1970 'The genesis of sport as a sociological problem', in Eric Dunning (ed.), *The Sociology of Sport*, London, Frank Cass, pp. 88–115.

1971 'Sociology of knowledge: new perspectives', *Sociology*, vol. 5, no. 2, pp. 149–68 and no. 3, pp. 355–70.

1972 'Theory of science and history of science: comments on a recent discussion', *Economy & Society*, vol. 1, no. 2, pp. 117–33.
'Processes of state formation and nation building', *Transactions of the 7th World Congress of Sociology, Varna, September 1970, Vol. 3*, Sofia: International Sociological Association, pp. 274–84.
'Dynamics of consciousness within that of societies', *Transactions of the 7th World Congress of Sociology, Varna, September 1970, Vol. 4*, Sofia: International Sociological Association, pp. 375–83.

1974 'The sciences: towards a theory', in Richard Whitley (ed.) *Social*

Processes of Scientific Development, London, Routledge & Kegan Paul, pp. 21–42.

'Towards a theory of communities', in Colin Bell and Howard Newby (eds), *The Sociology of Community: A Selection of Readings*, London, Frank Cass, pp. ix–xli.

1978 *What is Sociology?* London, Hutchinson [1970].

The Civilizing Process, Vol. 1: The History of Manners, New York: Urizen [1939].

'The civilizing process revisited: interview with Stanislas Fontaine', *Theory & Society*, vol. 5, no. 2, pp. 243–54.

1982 'Scientific establishments', in N. Elias, R. Whitley and H.G. Martins (eds), *Scientific Establishments and Hierarchies*, Dordrecht, Reidel, pp. 3–69.

The Civilizing Process, Vol. 2: Power and Civility, New York, Pantheon [1939].

1983 'Civilization and violence: on the state monopoly of physical violence and its infringements', *Telos*, vol. 54, pp. 134–54.

The Court Society, New York, Pantheon [1969].

1984 'Knowledge and power: an interview by Peter Ludes', in Nico Stehr and Volker Meja (eds), *Society and Knowledge*, London, Transaction, pp. 251–91.

'On the sociogenesis of sociology', *Amsterdams Sociologisch Tijdschrift*, vol. 11, no. 1, pp. 14–52.

1985 *The Loneliness of the Dying*, Oxford, Basil Blackwell [1982].

1986 *Quest for Excitement: Sport and Leisure in the Civilizing Process* [with Eric Dunning], Oxford, Basil Blackwell.

1987 'The changing balance of power between the sexes', *Theory, Culture & Society*, vol. 4, nos 2–3, pp. 287–316.

'On human beings and their emotions: a process-sociological essay', *Theory, Culture & Society*, vol. 4, nos 2–3, pp. 339–61.

'The retreat of sociologists into the present', in V. Meja, D. Misgeld and N. Stehr (eds), *Modern German Sociology*, New York, Columbia University Press, pp. 150–72 [1983].

Involvement and Detachment, Oxford, Basil Blackwell.

'On transformations of aggressiveness', *Theory & Society*, vol. 5, no. 2, pp. 227–53.

1991 *The Society of Individuals*, Oxford, Basil Blackwell. [1987]

The Symbol Theory, London, Sage.

1992 *Time: An Essay*, Oxford, Basil Blackwell [1984].

1993 *Mozart: Portrait of a Genius*, Cambridge, Polity [1991]

1994   *Reflections on a Life*, Cambridge, Polity Press [1987].
        The Civilizing Process, Oxford, Basil Blackwell [1939].

1995   'Technization and civilization', *Theory, Culture & Society*, vol. 12, no. 3, pp. 7–42 [1986].

1996   *The Germans*, Oxford, Basil Blackwell [1989].

1997/   'Towards a theory of social processes: a translation', *British Journal*
1988   *of Sociology*, vol. 48 (1997), pp. 355–83 [1977].

        'Idea and Individual', in *The Elias Reader: Selections From A Lifetime*, Johan Goudsblom and Stephen Mennell (eds), Oxford, Blackwell [1924].

        'On Primitive Art', in *The Elias Reader: Selections From A Lifetime*, Johan Goudsblom and Stephen Mennell (eds), Oxford, Blackwell [1929].

        'The Expulsion of the Huguenots from France', in *The Elias Reader*, Johan Goudsblom and Stephen Mennell (eds), Oxford, Blackwell [1935].

        'The Kitsch Style and the Age of Kitsch', in *The Elias Reader*, Johan Goudsblom and Stephen Mennell (eds), Oxford, Blackwell [1935].

        'Group Charisma and Group Disgrace', in *The Elias Reader*, Johan Goudsblom and Stephen Mennell (eds), Oxford, Blackwell [1964].

        'African Art', in *The Elias Reader*, Johan Goudsblom and Stephen Mennell (eds), Oxford, Blackwell [1970].

        'An Interview in Amsterdam, with Johan Goudsblom', in *The Elias Reader*, Johan Goudsblom and Stephen Mennell (eds), Oxford, Blackwell [1970].

        'On the Concept of Everyday Life', in *The Elias Reader*, Johan Goudsblom and Stephen Mennell (eds), Oxford, Blackwell [1978].

        'Renate Rubinstein', in *The Elias Reader*, Johan Goudsblom and Stephen Mennell (eds), Oxford. Blackwell [1980].

        'The Civilizing of Parents', in *The Elias Reader*, Johan Goudsblom and Stephen Mennell (eds), Oxford, Blackwell [1980], pp. 189–211.

INDEX